Chicken Dinners in ONE POT

Peggy Fallon

A John Boswell Associates/King Hill Productions Book
HarperCollins*Publishers*

HarperCollins books may be purchased for educational, business, or sales promotional use. For information please write: Special Markets Department, HarperCollins Publishers, Inc., 10 East 53rd Street, New York, NY 10022.

FIRST EDITION

Interior design by Stephanie Tevonian
Cover design by Suzanne Noli
Illustrations by John Jinks

Library of Congress Cataloging-in-Publication Data

Fallon, Peggy.
    Chicken dinners in one pot / Peggy Fallon. —1st ed.
        p.   cm.
    "A John Boswell Associates/King Hill Productions book."
    Includes index.
    ISBN 0-06-017316-5
    1. Cookery (Chicken)   2. Casserole cookery.   I. Title.
TX750.5.C45F35   1996   96-11148
641.6'65—dc20

97 98 99 00 01 HC 10 9 8 7 6 5 4 3 2 1

Many thanks to my
good friend Lonnie Gandara, who steered me in the
right direction and remains a loyal cheerleader.
Once again, to computer caretakers Marilyn Luebbert
and Leland Chin, who face each deadline with
good humor and enthusiasm. To Susan Wyler, my
editor, who keeps me on track. And especially to
JMG, who kept me in a fowl mood. I thank you.

Contents

Introduction

Whether simmered slowly or cooked with a single flash in the pan, one-pot suppers are a great choice for today's busy cooks. They offer an ease of preparation, simplicity of cooking, and minimum of cleanup ideally suited to our hectic contemporary lifestyle. And what could be better to fill that single pot than America's favorite bird?

Savvy Americans consume literally billions of pounds of chicken each year. Why? Primarily because it tastes so good. It's also economical, readily available, nutritious, quick, easy, and versatile to prepare; it also keeps well in the freezer. Many choose it because, compared to other meats, it is so low in saturated fat.

Since chicken has overtaken beef as the most frequently served meat on American tables, it's only natural to seek new ways to prepare it. No longer satisfied with the freezer-to-microwave philosophy of eating, today's cook knows the importance of delicious home-cooked meals made from fresh ingredients.

To meet the growing demand for variety in our diet, supermarkets now stock a dazzling array of chicken: whole roasters and fryers, thighs and breasts on or off the bone, chicken tenders, ground chicken, chicken drumsticks, drumettes, wings, gizzards. . . . Well, you get the picture.

Now more than just a sign of prosperity, "a chicken in every pot" means that supper is going to be a hit tonight. Whether it's a casual family dinner, a neighborhood potluck, or an elegant dinner party, chicken is always right at home on the range . . . or in the oven . . . or the clay pot . . . or the slow cooker . . . or the pressure cooker.

In this book, you will find a chicken recipe to cook in every pot of your "*batterie de cuisine.*" In fact, you will probably be inspired to reactivate a few pots that had been relegated to the back of a cupboard.

Each chapter begins with a description of the appropriate pot, followed by more than a dozen creative ideas for bringing fabulous, fuss-free, chicken one-dish suppers to your table.

Poultry Pointers

- When selecting a chicken, look for a plump, full-breasted bird with smooth, unblemished skin, a clean smell, and few pinfeathers.
- Before cooking, rinse the chicken thoroughly with cold water and pat dry with paper towels.
- Wash your hands with soap and water before and after handling raw poultry.
- Use hot soapy water to wash the cutting board, work surface, knife, or any other utensil that comes in contact with uncooked chicken.
- To freeze chicken, remove and discard the store's wrapping material and wrap lightly in heavy-duty foil, plastic wrap, or freezer wrap.
- Thaw poultry on a plate or tray in the refrigerator overnight.
- Discard any liquid used to marinate chicken; it should not be served as a sauce. If used to baste while baking or grilling, be sure raw liquid boils at least 2 to 3 minutes over high heat to kill any bacteria.
- Chicken should be cooked until it is white throughout but still juicy; the juices should run clear—with no trace of pink—when the thigh is pierced with a fork at the thickest point.

Chicken Skillet Suppers

The very name of this chapter immediately brings a series of images to mind: everything from a cowboy hunched over the campfire with his trusty cast-iron skillet to a gingham-clad mom feeding her family from the stainless steel pans she received as a wedding gift. Not to mention a tony chef with a high toque, juggling his sauté pan over a high flame.

For all intents and purposes, a skillet is the same as a frying pan—a shallow round pan with a long handle and straight or flared sides that is used for stovetop cooking. Because of the design, its large flat surface comes directly in contact with the heat source, enabling it to cook a goodly amount of food at once. A skillet sometimes comes with its own lid, which is handy for braising after an initial browning. If your skillet doesn't have a lid, "universal lids," which fit a wide variety of pans, are sold at cookware shops.

Skillets run the gamut from expensive hammered French copper to flimsy dime-store enamelware. Whether you shop at a department store, cookware shop, or restaurant supply store, the most important thing is to purchase a heavy-bottomed pan that will not warp and will conduct heat evenly. Don't get side-tracked by the cute little pink pan with the mushrooms dancing across the handle. Beauty fades . . . sometimes faster than you'd ever anticipate.

A good skillet is a modest investment that will last a lifetime. Opt for a nonreactive pan; i.e., one that will not discolor or produce an off taste with acidic foods like tomatoes, green beans, spinach, or wine. This includes stainless steel, enameled cast iron, and certain bonded-nickel and aluminum pans. Tin is too flimsy and aluminum will react with foods too readily. Cast-iron skillets are great for a lot of things, but because the iron can react if not very well seasoned, they have their limitations when preparing one-pot meals.

You'll want a 10- or 12-inch pan for most skillet suppers. My personal favorite? A handsome 12-inch ovenproof skillet with 3-inch straight sides, a nonstick interior, a heatproof handle, and a glass lid. It is made by a national producer of quality commercial and home cookware and is sold as a "chicken fryer." I bought this skillet at a discount store a year ago for $20. Since that day this skillet has lived most of its life on my stove. Every time I think about putting it in the cupboard, I immediately find another use for it.

One reason this chapter is the largest in the book is that skillet suppers are so convenient because, by and large, they are so quick. In many instances you can have a tasty one-pot supper on the table in half an hour or less. The other reason is the unbelievable versatility of the humble skillet.

Travel around the world with Sautéed Chicken in Mango Chutney Sauce, Poached Chicken with Apples and Calvados, and Chicken Thighs Balsamico. Choose a quick Chicken Scaloppine or the hearty Cheesy Spanish Rice with Chicken and Black Beans.

Most dishes, like Herbed Chicken with Potatoes and Tomatoes, deliver a substantial meal-in-a-skillet. Lighter recipes, like Mellow Yellow Chicken with Vegetables, can be stretched by adding a side of steaming hot rice, if you feel it's needed. Otherwise, just a basket of good crusty bread and a green salad will round out the menu.

Poached Chicken with Apples and Calvados

*C**ooking with apples, Calvados, and cream is typical of the regions of Normandy and Brittany in France. Look for crème fraîche in the dairy section of your local supermarket or gourmet shop. If it is not available, substitute sour cream.* **Makes 6 servings**

2 cups apple juice
3 medium tart green apples, such
   as Granny Smith (about
   1 pound), peeled, cored, and cut
   into ½-inch wedges
3 medium leeks (white and tender
   green), halved lengthwise,
   rinsed well, and cut into ½-inch
   pieces
6 skinless, boneless chicken
   breast halves (about
   2¼ pounds)

¾ teaspoon salt
¾ teaspoon pepper, preferably
   white
3 cups chicken broth
⅓ cup Calvados or other apple
   brandy
3 tablespoons unsalted butter
2 tablespoons minced shallots
2 tablespoons flour
½ cup crème fraîche or sour
   cream
3 tablespoons minced chives

1) In a 12-inch nonreactive skillet, bring the apple juice to a simmer over medium heat. Add the apples and leeks and simmer, stirring occasionally, until just softened, 3 to 5 minutes. Using a slotted spoon, transfer the apples and leeks to a medium bowl and set aside.

2) Increase the heat to high and bring the apple juice to a boil. Cook until thickened and reduced to about ¼ cup, 5 to 7 minutes. Pour into a 2-cup glass measure and set aside.

3) Rinse the chicken under cold running water and pat dry. Season with the salt and pepper. Arrange the chicken breasts in a single layer in the skillet. Pour in the chicken broth and Calvados, partially cover, and bring to a simmer over medium-low heat. Cook until the chicken is white throughout but still juicy, 8 to 10 minutes. Remove the chicken and set aside.

4) Increase the heat to high and boil the liquid until thickened and reduced to about 1½ cups, 6 to 8 minutes. Add the liquid from the skillet to the reduced apple juice.

5) Add the butter to the skillet and heat over medium heat until melted. Add the shallots and cook until softened, 1 to 2 minutes. Whisk in the flour and cook, stirring, 1 to 2 minutes longer without allowing to color. Whisk in the reserved apple juice and poaching liquid and bring to a boil, whisking until thickened, 3 to 5 minutes.

6) Reduce the heat to low and whisk the crème fraîche into the sauce. Return the leeks, apples, and chicken to the skillet and turn to coat with the sauce. Cook until just heated through, about 2 minutes. (Do not let the sauce boil.) Sprinkle with the chopped chives just before serving.

Apricot-Glazed Chicken with Rice Pilaf

*T**his sweet and savory combo
needs only a crisp green salad to round out the meal.*

Makes 4 servings

1 (3½-pound) chicken, cut into
  8 pieces
1 teaspoon salt
½ teaspoon pepper
2 tablespoons vegetable oil
1 tablespoon butter
1 small onion, chopped

1¾ cups chicken broth
1 (6.09-ounce) package rice pilaf
  mix
⅓ cup chopped dried apricots
3 tablespoons apricot jam
1 tablespoon Dijon mustard

1) Rinse the chicken under cold running water and pat dry. Season with
the salt and pepper. In a 12-inch nonreactive skillet, heat the oil over medium
heat. Add the chicken and cook, turning, until nicely browned, about 10
minutes. Remove the chicken and set aside. Drain the fat from the pan.

2) In the same skillet, melt the butter over medium heat. Add the onion
and cook, stirring occasionally, until softened but not browned, 3 to 5 minutes.
Add the chicken broth and bring to a boil over medium heat, scraping up any
brown bits from the bottom of the pan. Stir in the pilaf mix, the contents of the
seasoning packet from the mix, and the apricots. Return the chicken to the pan
and return the liquid to a boil.

3) Meanwhile, mix the jam and mustard in a small bowl until well blended.
Brush or spoon the jam mixture over the chicken pieces. Reduce the heat to
medium-low, cover, and cook until the rice pilaf is tender, most of the liquid
has been absorbed, and the chicken is white throughout but still juicy, 20 to 30
minutes.

Chicken Thighs Balsamico

T*he ingredients here highlight the sweet-tart flavor of balsamic vinegar. This dish is great for summer entertaining, since it can be served at room temperature. Just add a basket of good Italian bread. Because in this recipe vinegar boils directly in the pan, be sure to use a nonreactive skillet.*

Makes 4 servings

8 to 10 chicken thighs (2 to 2½ pounds)
½ teaspoon salt
¼ teaspoon pepper
2 tablespoons olive oil
½ cup balsamic vinegar
2 tablespoons Dijon mustard
1 cup chicken broth

¼ cup dried currants or raisins
1 tablespoon chopped fresh marjoram or 1 teaspoon dried
1 tablespoon grated lemon or orange zest
¼ teaspoon sugar (optional)
½ pound arugula or curly endive

1) Rinse the chicken under cold running water and pat dry. Season with the salt and pepper. In a 12-inch nonreactive skillet, heat the olive oil over medium-high heat. Add the chicken and cook, turning occasionally, until nicely browned outside and white throughout but still juicy, 15 to 18 minutes. Remove the chicken and set aside. Drain off all the fat from the pan.

2) Add the vinegar to the same skillet and bring to a boil over medium-high heat, scraping up any browned bits from the bottom of the pan. Whisk in the mustard until well blended. Add the broth and currants and cook, whisking constantly, until thickened to the consistency of syrup, about 2 minutes. Stir in the marjoram and 2 teaspoons of the lemon zest and cook 1 minute longer. If the sauce is too acidic for your liking, add the sugar.

3) Just before serving, line a platter with the arugula and top with the chicken thighs. Spoon a little sauce over each piece of chicken and sprinkle the remaining 1 teaspoon lemon zest on top. Serve warm or at room temperature.

Cheesy Spanish Rice with Chicken and Black Beans

Thisenergy-packed entrée is perfect for casual family suppers. Though the rice makes a satisfying meal in itself, you can serve it with warm flour tortillas for make-it-yourself burritos. Converted rice keeps its shape during cooking, making a more attractive dish.

Makes 4 to 6 servings

1 tablespoon vegetable oil
1 pound ground chicken
1 medium onion, chopped
1 jalapeño or serrano pepper, seeded and minced
1 garlic clove, minced
1 cup converted long-grain white rice
1 (28-ounce) can diced tomatoes, juices reserved
1 (6-ounce) can tomato paste
1 cup chicken broth

1 (4-ounce) can diced green chiles
1 teaspoon ground cumin
1 teaspoon chili powder
¾ teaspoon salt
¼ teaspoon pepper
1 (15-ounce) can black beans, rinsed and drained
1 (11-ounce) can corn kernels, drained
1 cup shredded Cheddar cheese (about 4 ounces)
Sour cream and salsa

1) In a 12-inch nonreactive skillet, heat the oil over medium-high heat. Add the chicken, onion, jalapeño pepper, and garlic. Cook, stirring to break up the meat, until the chicken has lost all trace of pink and the vegetables are softened, about 7 minutes. Drain off the excess fat from the pan.

2) Stir in the rice, tomatoes with their juices, tomato paste, chicken broth, chiles, cumin, chili powder, salt, and pepper. Bring to a boil, stirring occasionally. Reduce the heat to low, cover, and cook until the rice is tender, about 30 minutes.

3) Stir in the beans and corn and continue cooking, covered, until the beans and corn are heated through, 3 to 5 minutes. Just before serving, stir in the cheese. Pass the sour cream and salsa at the table.

Skillet Stew Santa Fe

Not all stews need to simmer for hours—this one goes together in a jiffy. Serve with warm tortillas, sour cream, and shredded Cheddar cheese for a perfectly satisfying meal. ***Makes 4 to 6 servings***

3 skinless, boneless chicken
  breast halves (about 1 pound)
¾ teaspoon salt
2 tablespoons vegetable oil
1 large onion, chopped
3 garlic cloves, minced
1½ teaspoons chili powder
½ teaspoon ground cumin
⅛ teaspoon cayenne
1 (15-ounce) can red kidney
  beans, rinsed and drained

1 (15-ounce) can black beans,
  rinsed and drained
1 (14½-ounce) can stewed
  tomatoes, juices reserved
1 (11-ounce) can corn kernels,
  drained
1 (4-ounce) can diced green chiles
3 tablespoons coarsely chopped
  cilantro

1) Rinse the chicken under cold running water and pat dry. Cut into ¾-inch pieces and season with the salt. In a 12-inch nonreactive skillet, heat 1 tablespoon of the oil over medium-high heat. Add the chicken and cook, stirring occasionally, until nicely browned outside and white throughout but still juicy, 3 to 4 minutes. Remove the chicken and set aside.

2) Reduce the heat to medium and heat the remaining 1 tablespoon oil in the same skillet. Add the onion, garlic, chili powder, cumin, and cayenne and cook, stirring occasionally, until the onion is softened but not browned, 3 to 5 minutes.

3) Stir in the kidney beans, black beans, tomatoes with their juices, corn, and chiles and bring to a boil over high heat. Reduce the heat to medium and cook until mixture is thickened slightly, 10 to 15 minutes.

4) Stir in the chicken and cilantro and cook until heated through, about 5 minutes longer. Season with additional salt and pepper to taste.

Chicken with Broccoli and Rapid Rice

This meal can be put together in no time if you use chicken tenders and cut-up broccoli from a supermarket salad bar.

Makes 4 servings

4 skinless, boneless chicken
  breast halves (about
  1½ pounds)
1 teaspoon sugar
½ teaspoon grated fresh ginger
3 tablespoons soy sauce
2 teaspoons cornstarch
1 garlic clove, minced
⅛ teaspoon crushed hot red
  pepper
1 tablespoon peanut or vegetable
  oil

1 cup chicken broth
¾ cup quick-cooking long-grain
  white rice
1 pound broccoli florets, cut in
  1-inch pieces
1 small red bell pepper, cut into
  ½-inch squares
1 scallion, cut diagonally into
  ½-inch lengths

1) Rinse the chicken under cold running water and pat dry. Cut across the grain into thin strips. In a medium bowl or a heavy-duty 1-gallon plastic bag, combine the sugar, ginger, soy sauce, cornstarch, garlic, and crushed red pepper. Add the chicken strips and toss well to mix. Let stand at room temperature 15 minutes.

2) In a 12-inch nonreactive skillet, heat the oil over high heat. Add the chicken and cook, stirring occasionally, until the chicken is white throughout but still juicy, 3 to 5 minutes. Remove the chicken and set aside.

3) Add the chicken broth, rice, and broccoli to the skillet and bring to a boil over high heat. Reduce the heat to medium-low, cover, and simmer until the broccoli is crisp-tender, about 5 minutes.

4) Increase the heat to high and return the chicken to the skillet. Add the bell pepper and scallion and cook, stirring and tossing, 2 minutes longer to soften the pepper slightly. Serve hot.

Chicken Chardonnay with Aromatic Vegetables

Makes 4 servings

1 (3½-pound) chicken, cut into
  8 pieces
1 teaspoon salt
¼ teaspoon pepper
2 tablespoons olive oil
2 medium onions, halved
  lengthwise and cut into slices
  ½ inch thick
2 carrots, peeled and cut into
  ½-inch dice

2 celery ribs, cut into ½-inch dice
2 large garlic cloves, minced
1 cup chicken broth
½ cup Chardonnay or other dry
  white wine
1 bay leaf
½ cup heavy cream (optional)
2 tablespoons chopped parsley

1) Rinse the chicken under cold running water and pat dry. Season with the salt and pepper. In a 12-inch nonreactive skillet, heat the oil over medium heat. Add the chicken and cook, turning, until nicely browned, about 10 minutes. Remove the chicken and set aside.

2) Pour off and discard all but 2 tablespoons of the fat left in the pan. Add the onions and cook, stirring occasionally, until just softened, about 2 minutes. Add the carrots, celery, and garlic and cook, stirring occasionally, until softened, about 5 minutes.

3) Add the chicken broth, wine, and bay leaf. Bring to a boil over medium-high heat, scraping up any brown bits from the bottom of the pan. Return the chicken to the skillet and bring to a boil. Reduce the heat to medium-low, cover, and simmer until the chicken is white throughout but still juicy, 20 to 30 minutes.

4) Remove and discard the bay leaf. With tongs, transfer the chicken to a warm serving platter. If using the cream, add to the sauce and cook over medium-high heat, stirring, until slightly thickened, 3 to 5 minutes. Pour the sauce over the chicken and garnish with the parsley.

Chicken Breasts with Creamy Linguine

Here's another one-pot pasta that requires little more than a green salad and garlic bread to make a delightful meal.

Makes 4 servings

4 skinless, boneless chicken
  breast halves (about
  1½ pounds)
1 teaspoon salt
½ teaspoon pepper
½ teaspoon paprika
1 tablespoon butter
1 tablespoon olive oil
1 onion, cut into slices about
  ¼ inch thick
2 garlic cloves, minced

1 cup chicken broth
1 (14½-ounce) can diced
  tomatoes, juices reserved
⅓ cup heavy cream
4 ounces linguine, broken into
  thirds (pieces about 3 inches
  long)
1 tablespoon chopped fresh basil
  or parsley plus a few leaves or
  sprigs for garnish
⅛ teaspoon cayenne

1) Rinse the chicken under cold running water and pat dry. Season with the salt, pepper, and paprika.

2) In a deep 12-inch nonreactive skillet, melt the butter in the olive oil over medium heat. Add the chicken and cook, turning, until lightly browned, 4 to 6 minutes. Remove the chicken and set aside.

3) Add the onion and garlic to the skillet and cook, stirring occasionally, until softened but not browned, 3 to 5 minutes. Add the chicken broth, tomatoes with their juices, and cream and bring to a boil. Stir in the linguine, basil, and cayenne and return to a boil. Reduce the heat to medium-low, return the chicken to the skillet, and cover. Cook until the chicken is white throughout but still juicy and the pasta is tender, about 15 minutes.

4) With tongs, transfer the chicken to a warm serving platter. Increase the heat to medium-high and boil until the sauce is slightly thickened, 1 to 2 minutes. Surround the chicken with the pasta and drizzle with any sauce remaining in the pan. Garnish with leaves or sprigs of fresh basil.

Sautéed Chicken in Mango Chutney Sauce

*G*aram masala is an aromatic blend of spices often used in Indian curries. Look for it in well-stocked supermarkets, Indian markets, and shops that specialize in dried herbs and spices.

Makes 4 servings

1 (3½-pound) chicken, cut into
  8 pieces, rinsed and patted dry
1 teaspoon salt
1 teaspoon garam masala or
  ½ teaspoon ground cumin and
  ⅛ teaspoon cinnamon
2 tablespoons vegetable oil
1 large tart green apple, peeled
  and cut into ¾-inch chunks
1 medium onion, coarsely
  chopped
1 celery rib, coarsely chopped

1 tablespoon curry powder
1½ tablespoons flour
½ cup orange juice
½ cup chicken broth
Grated zest of 1 lime
½ cup finely chopped mango
  chutney
½ cup dried cranberries or raisins
Dash of cayenne
1 scallion, thinly sliced
Lime wedges

1) Season the chicken with the salt and garam masala. In a 12-inch nonreactive skillet, heat the oil over medium heat. Add the chicken and cook, turning, until nicely browned, about 10 minutes. Remove the chicken and set aside. Drain off and discard all but 2 tablespoons of the fat from the pan.

2) Add the apple, onion, and celery to the skillet and cook over medium heat, stirring occasionally, until softened but not browned, 3 to 5 minutes. Add the curry powder and flour and cook, stirring constantly, 1 minute longer.

3) Add the orange juice, chicken broth, and lime zest. Bring to a boil over medium-high heat, scraping up any browned bits from the bottom of the pan. Stir in the chutney, cranberries, and cayenne. Return the chicken to the skillet and bring to a boil. Reduce the heat to medium-low, cover, and simmer until the chicken is white throughout but still juicy, 20 to 30 minutes. Just before serving, sprinkle on the scallion and garnish with lime wedges.

Chicken and Vegetables Marinara

Besides having a lot of traditional Italian flavor, this skillet supper carries the unexpected zing of goat cheese. With or without pasta, it's a great dish for entertaining.

Makes 4 to 6 servings

6 skinless, boneless chicken
   breast halves (about
   2¼ pounds)
1 teaspoon salt
½ teaspoon pepper
3 tablespoons olive oil
1 medium onion, chopped
3 medium zucchini, cut into
   ½-inch dice
¼ pound mushrooms, halved
1 small green bell peper, cut into
   ½-inch squares

4 garlic cloves, minced
1 (14½-ounce) can diced peeled
   tomatoes, drained, juices
   reserved
1½ cups marinara sauce
   (purchased or homemade)
1 tablespoon red wine vinegar
1½ teapoons chopped fresh
   marjoram or ½ teaspoon dried
½ cup crumbled goat cheese
   (about 2 ounces)
3 tablespoons chopped parsley

1) Rinse the chicken under cold running water and pat dry. Season with the salt and pepper. Heat 2 tablespoons of the olive oil in a 12-inch nonreactive skillet over medium-high heat. Add the chicken and cook, turning, until lightly browned but not completely cooked through, about 5 minutes. Remove the chicken and set aside.

2) Heat the remaining 1 tablespoon olive oil in the same skillet over medium-high heat. And the onion and cook, stirring occasionally, until just
   softened, 2 to 3 minutes. Add the zucchini, mushrooms, bell pepper, and garlic. Cook, stirring often, until the vegetables are crisp-tender, 3 to 5 minutes longer. Stir in the tomatoes but not their juices and cook until most of the liquid has evaporated, about 3 minutes. Using a slotted spoon, remove the vegetable mixture from the skillet and set aside.

3) Add the marinara sauce, ½ cup of the reserved tomato juices, the vinegar, and marjoram to the skillet. Bring to a boil and reduce the heat to medium-low. Add the chicken breasts and turn to coat with the sauce. Cook until the chicken is white throughout but still juicy, 8 to 10 minutes.

4) Transfer the chicken to a warm serving platter. Return the vegetable mixture to the sauce and cook over medium heat until heated through, about 2 minutes. Using a slotted spoon, arrange the vegetables around the chicken breasts. Spoon the hot sauce over all and sprinkle with the goat cheese and parsley.

Chicken with Mushrooms, Spinach, and Bulgur

*C*racked wheat bulgur has a *pleasantly nutty flavor and a somewhat chewy texture. Although it can be purchased in bulk, you will also find it in 1-pound boxes at the supermarket. Serve with pita bread for impromptu sandwich making. To save time, use a 12-ounce bag of ready-to-use trimmed and washed spinach, if it is available in your market.*

Makes 4 servings

2 tablespoons pine nuts (pignoli)
1 pound fresh spinach leaves, well
   rinsed and coarsely chopped
   (about 3 cups)
2 tablespoons olive oil
½ pound mushrooms, sliced
1 pound ground chicken
1 medium onion, chopped

1 small red or green bell pepper,
   cut into ½-inch squares
2 garlic cloves, minced
1 teaspoon salt
½ teaspoon ground cumin
1 cup bulgur
2 cups chicken broth

1) In a dry 12-inch nonreactive skillet, toast the pine nuts over medium heat, stirring constantly, until lightly browned, 2 to 3 minutes. Remove the nuts from the skillet and set aside to cool.

2) Add the spinach and any water that clings to the leaves to the same skillet. Cover and cook over medium-high heat until the spinach is wilted but still bright green and the water has evaporated, 2 to 3 minutes. Drain the spinach and rinse under cold running water; squeeze to remove the excess liquid.

3) In the same skillet, heat 1 tablespoon of the olive oil over medium heat. Add the mushrooms and cook, stirring occasionally, until they give up their juices and the liquid evaporates, 5 to 7 minutes. Remove the mushrooms with a slotted spoon.

4) Add the remaining 1 tablespoon olive oil to the skillet and heat over medium heat. Add the chicken, onion, bell pepper, garlic, salt, and cumin. Cook, stirring to break up the meat, until the chicken has lost all trace of pink and the vegetables are softened, about 7 minutes. Add the spinach, mushrooms, and bulgur and cook, stirring constantly, until the spinach wilts, 1 minute longer.

5) Add the chicken broth and bring to a boil, scraping up any brown bits from the bottom of the pan. Reduce the heat to low, cover, and cook until the bulgur is tender and most of the liquid has been absorbed, about 15 minutes. Sprinkle with the toasted pine nuts just before serving.

Mustard-Braised Chicken Thighs

This quickly assembled meal is great for busy days because it features ingredients that can be kept in your freezer and pantry.

Makes 4 servings

4 large red potatoes (about 1½ pounds), scrubbed and cut into ¾-inch dice
4 bacon slices (about ¼ pound), cut into ½-inch pieces
8 skinless, boneless chicken thighs (about 1¼ pounds)
½ teaspoon salt
¼ teaspoon pepper
1 tablespoon olive oil

1½ tablespoons whole-grain mustard
1 cup chicken broth
1 (10-ounce) bag frozen petite whole (pearl) onions, thawed
1 (9-ounce) package frozen Italian green beans, thawed
1½ teaspoons chopped fresh thyme leaves or ½ teaspoon dried leaves

1) In a 12-inch nonreactive skillet half full of boiling salted water, cook the potatoes until barely tender, about 4 minutes. Drain the potatoes and carefully wipe out the pan.

2) In the same skillet, cook the bacon over medium heat until browned and crisp, 4 to 5 minutes. Using a slotted spoon, transfer the bacon to paper towels to drain. Pour off the bacon drippings from the pan.

3) Rinse the chicken under cold running water and pat dry. Season with the salt and pepper. In the same skillet, heat the olive oil over medium-high heat. Add the chicken and cook, turning, until nicely browned, about 4 minutes. Reduce the heat to low. Move the chicken to the side of the skillet and whisk the mustard and chicken broth into the pan juices until well blended.

4) Add the potatoes and onions and toss with the chicken. Cover and cook until the potatoes are tender and the chicken is white throughout but still juicy, about 15 minutes.

5) Add the bacon, green beans, and thyme. Cook, uncovered, stirring occasionally, until the sauce is slightly thickened, 5 to 7 minutes.

Divine Divan with Oodles O' Noodles

Dishes like Chicken Divan enjoyed a wild spate of popularity at ladies' luncheons in the 1950s. Now such entrées have been relegated to the freezer section of your local supermarket. Here's a tasty twist on an old theme.

Makes 4 to 6 servings

2 skinless, boneless chicken breast halves (about ¾ pound)
¾ teaspoon salt
2 tablespoons unsalted butter
1 teaspoon vegetable oil
1 tablespoon minced shallot
1 bunch of fresh broccoli, coarsely chopped (about 4 cups)

Dash of grated nutmeg
Dash of cayenne
1¾ cups chicken broth
1 cup half-and-half
6 ounces medium egg noodles (about 3 cups)
⅓ cup grated Parmesan cheese

1) Rinse the chicken under cold running water and pat dry. Cut into ¾-inch pieces and season with ¼ teaspoon of the salt. In a deep 12-inch nonreactive skillet, melt 1 tablespoon of the butter in the oil over medium heat. Add the shallot and cook, stirring occasionally, until softened but not browned, 1 to 2 minutes. Add the chicken and cook, stirring often, until lightly browned outside and white throughout but still juicy, 3 to 4 minutes. Remove the chicken and set aside.

2) Add the remaining 1 tablespoon butter to the skillet and melt over medium heat. Add the broccoli and cook, tossing, 1 to 2 minutes. Season with the remaining ½ teaspoon salt, the nutmeg, and cayenne.

3) Stir in the chicken broth, half-and-half, and uncooked noodles. Bring to a boil over medium-high heat, then reduce the heat to low. Stir in the chicken, cover, and cook until the noodles are tender but still firm, 25 to 30 minutes. Sprinkle with the Parmesan cheese and serve at once.

Chicken with Greek Olives and Cheese

*T*he lusty flavors of this sauce
require a crusty loaf of coarse, country-style white bread for
maximum enjoyment.   ***Makes 4 servings***

1 (3½-pound) chicken, cut into
   8 pieces
5 tablespoons fresh lemon juice
5 tablespoons olive oil
1½ tablespoons chopped fresh
   oregano or 1½ teaspoons dried
3 garlic cloves, minced
¼ teaspoon pepper
Salt
1 medium onion, cut into slices
   ¼ inch thick

1 cup chicken broth
1 (14½-ounce) can diced peeled
   tomatoes, drained
16 kalamata olives (about ⅓ cup),
   pitted
Dash of cayenne
4 ounces feta cheese
Oregano sprigs and lemon wedges

1) Rinse the chicken under cold running water and pat dry. Place the chicken in a heavy-duty 1-gallon plastic bag. Add 3 tablespoons of the lemon juice, 3 tablespoons of the olive oil, 1 tablespoon of the oregano, the garlic, and pepper. Seal the bag securely and turn several times to coat the chicken. Let stand 1 hour at room temperature. Remove the chicken, pat dry, and season with salt. Discard any leftover marinade.

2) In a 12-inch nonreactive skillet, heat the remaining 2 tablespoons olive oil over medium heat. Add the chicken and cook, turning, until nicely browned, about 10 minutes. Remove the chicken from the skillet and set aside. Drain off all but 2 teaspoons of the fat from the pan.

3) Add the onion to the skillet and cook, stirring occasionally, until softened but not browned, 3 to 5 minutes. Whisk in the remaining 2 tablespoons lemon juice and the chicken broth. Bring to a boil over medium-high heat, scraping up any brown bits from the bottom of the pan. Stir in the tomatoes, olives, and cayenne.

4) Return the chicken to the skillet and bring to a boil. Reduce the heat to medium-low, cover, and cook until the chicken is white throughout but still juicy, 20 to 30 minutes. Using a slotted spoon, transfer the chicken and olives to a warm serving platter. Increase the heat to medium-high and cook until the sauce has thickened slightly, about 5 minutes.

5) Crumble the feta cheese over the chicken and cover with the warm sauce. Sprinkle with the remaining 1½ teaspoons oregano. Garnish with the oregano springs and lemon wedges. Serve at once.

Italian Chicken with Green Olives and Rosemary

T*his sauce is wonderful with crusty Italian rolls and heavenly over polenta.* **Makes 4 servings**

1 (3½-pound) chicken, cut into
  8 pieces
¾ teaspoon salt
¼ teaspoon pepper
2 tablespoons olive oil
1 medium onion, chopped
3 garlic cloves, minced
1 (14½-ounce) can diced Italian-
  seasoned tomatoes, drained

1 cup dry white wine
1 cup chicken broth
16 pitted or pimiento-stuffed
  green olives (about ½ cup)
1½ tablespoons chopped fresh
  rosemary or 1½ teaspoons dried

1) Rinse the chicken under cold running water and pat dry. Season with the salt and pepper. In a 12-inch skillet, heat the olive oil over medium heat. Add the chicken and cook, turning, until nicely browned, about 10 minutes. Remove the chicken and set aside. Drain off all but 1 tablespoon of the fat from the pan.

2) Add the onion to the skillet and cook over medium heat, stirring occasionally, until softened but not browned, 3 to 5 minutes. Add the garlic and cook until just fragrant, about 1 minute. Stir in the tomatoes, wine, chicken broth, and 1 cup water. Bring to a boil over medium-high heat, scraping up any browned bits from the bottom of the pan. Return the chicken to the skillet and bring to a boil. Reduce the heat to medium-low, cover, and cook 15 minutes.

3) Add the olives and 1 tablespoon of the rosemary to the pan, cover, and cook until the chicken is white throughout but still juicy, 5 to 15 minutes longer. Using a slotted spoon, transfer the chicken and olives to a warm serving platter and cover with foil to keep warm.

4) Increase the heat to medium-high and cook, stirring often, until the sauce is thickened and reduced to about 2¼ cups, 6 to 8 minutes. Pour the sauce over the chicken and sprinkle with the remaining 1½ teaspoons rosemary.

Spiced Chicken in Orange Sauce

Basmati or wild rice makes a *fitting complement to this sweet and spicy sauce.*

Makes 6 servings

½ cup slivered almonds
6 skinless, boneless chicken breast halves (5 to 6 ounces each)
1 teaspoon salt
1 teaspoon curry powder
¼ teaspoon pepper
4 tablespoons unsalted butter
2 tablespoons flour
¼ teaspoon cinnamon

¼ teaspoon ground ginger
1½ cups orange juice
1 (10-ounce) jar orange marmalade
2 tablespoons brandy
2 (11-ounce) cans mandarin orange segments, drained
½ cup golden raisins
1 bunch of watercress

1) In a dry 12-inch skillet, toast the almonds over medium heat, stirring occasionally, until lightly browned, 3 to 4 minutes. Remove the almonds and set aside to cool.

2) Rinse the chicken under cold running water and pat dry. Season with the salt, curry powder, and pepper. Add 2 tablespoons of the butter to the same skillet and melt over medium heat. Add the chicken and cook, turning, until nicely browned outside and white throughout but still juicy, 6 to 8 minutes. Transfer the chicken to a warm serving platter.

3) Melt the remaining 2 tablespoons butter in the same skillet over medium heat. Add the flour, cinnamon, and ginger and cook, stirring constantly, 1 minute.

4) Whisk in the orange juice and bring to a boil, scraping up any brown bits from the bottom of the pan. Reduce the heat to medium-low and cook, stirring constantly, until slightly thickened, 1 to 2 minutes. Stir in the marmalade and brandy. Add the orange segments and raisins and cook until heated through, 2 to 3 minutes longer. To serve, spoon the sauce over the chicken breasts and sprinkle with the almonds. Garnish with the watercress.

Piquant Chicken with Vegetables al Pesto

*T*he gutsy flavor of pesto makes this dinner anything but ordinary. Panzanella, the classic Tuscan bread salad, would be an excellent first course. ***Makes 4 servings***

4 skinless, boneless chicken
   breast halves (about
   1½ pounds)
1½ tablespoons fresh lemon juice
4 teaspoons olive oil
¾ teaspoon salt
1 garlic clove, minced
¼ teaspoon pepper
¾ pound small red potatoes,
   scrubbed and cut into slices
   about ½ inch thick

¾ pound green beans, trimmed
   and cut into 1½-inch lengths
1 tablespoon butter
16 kalamata olives (about ⅓ cup),
   pitted and coarsely chopped
¾ cup pesto sauce, purchased or
   homemade (page 138)
Fresh basil sprigs

1) Rinse the chicken under cold running water and pat dry. Pound the chicken breasts between 2 sheets of wax paper until flattened evenly to a ¼-inch thickness. Season with the lemon juice, 2 teaspoons of the olive oil, the salt, garlic, and pepper.

2) Fill a 10- or 12-inch nonreactive skillet two-thirds full with salted water and bring to a boil over high heat. Add the potatoes and cook until barely tender, about 4 minutes. Add the green beans and continue to cook until the potatoes are tender and the green beans are crisp-tender, 4 to 6 minutes longer. Drain, discarding the cooking water.

3) In the same skillet, melt the butter in the remaining 2 teaspoons olive oil over medium heat. Add the chicken and cook, turning, until nicely browned outside and white throughout but still juicy, 4 to 6 minutes. With tongs, transfer the chicken breasts to a warm serving platter, overlapping them slightly. Cover loosely with aluminum foil to keep warm.

4) Return the potatoes and green beans to the skillet. Add half of the olives. Cook over medium-high heat, gently stirring to coat with the pan juices, until heated through, about 2 minutes. Remove from the heat. Add the pesto and toss to coat the vegetables.

5) Spoon the potato and green bean mixture around the chicken breasts. Scatter the remaining olives over the chicken and garnish with sprigs of fresh basil.

Chicken Breasts Peperonata

*A**ssemble this colorful creation in late summer or early fall when the peppers and vine-ripened tomatoes are cheap and plentiful. It's a great choice for warm-weather entertaining since it is equally delicious at room temperature.*

Makes 4 to 6 servings

6 skinless, boneless chicken breast halves (about 2¼ pounds)
1 teaspooon salt
½ teaspoon pepper
¼ cup olive oil
3 large garlic cloves, thinly sliced
1 large onion, cut into slices about ¼ inch thick
3 large bell peppers, preferably 2 red and 1 yellow, cut into strips about ¼ inch wide

2 tablespoons balsamic or sherry wine vinegar
3 large tomatoes, peeled, seeded, and coarsely chopped, or 1 (14½-ounce) can diced tomatoes, drained
2 tablespoons drained capers
3 tablespoons chopped parsley

1) Rinse the chicken under cold running water and pat dry. Season with the salt and pepper. Heat the olive oil in a 12-inch nonreactive skillet over medium heat. Add the chicken and cook, turning until nicely browned outside and white throughout but still juicy, 7 to 9 minutes. Remove the chicken to a plate and cover loosely with aluminum foil to keep warm.

2) Add the garlic and onion to the skillet and cook until softened and fragrant, about 2 minutes. Add the bell peppers and cook, stirring occasionally, until the peppers are bright in color and softened, 3 to 5 minutes longer.

3) Stir in the vinegar and tomatoes. Increase the heat to medium-high and cook until the juices thicken slightly, 2 to 3 minutes. Remove the skillet from the heat and stir in the capers and 2 tablespoons of the parsley. Season with additional salt and pepper to taste. Transfer the pepper mixture to a warm platter and top with the chicken breasts. Garnish with the remaining 1 tablespoon parsley. Serve warm or at room temperature.

Chicken Breasts with Port and Mushroom Sauce

To create a menu suitable for entertaining, simply serve this rich and sophisticated supper over wild rice. **Makes 4 servings**

4 skinless, boneless chicken
   breast halves
3 tablespoons flour
1 teaspoon salt
½ teaspoon pepper
¼ teaspoon grated nutmeg
4 tablespoons unsalted butter
2 tablespoons chopped shallots

½ pound mushrooms, sliced
½ cup tawny port
1 teaspoon lemon juice
½ cup chicken broth
½ cup heavy cream
2 teaspoons chopped fresh
   tarragon or parsley plus 4 sprigs
   for garnish

1) Rinse the chicken under cold running water and pat dry. Pound the chicken breasts between 2 sheets of wax paper until flattened evenly to a ½-inch thickness. Combine the flour, salt, pepper, and nutmeg in a shallow dish. Add the chicken and turn to coat evenly on both sides.

2) In a 12-inch nonreactive skillet, melt 2 tablespoons of the butter over medium-high heat. Add the chicken and cook, turning, until lightly browned outside and white throughout but still juicy, 6 to 8 minutes. Transfer the chicken to a warm platter and cover loosely with foil to keep warm.

3) Reduce the heat to medium. Melt the remaining 2 tablespoons butter in the skillet. Add the shallots and cook until softened, 1 to 2 minutes. Add the mushrooms and cook, stirring occasionally, until the mushrooms are tender and the liquid they exude evaporates, about 3 to 5 minutes.

4) Add the port and lemon juice to the skillet and bring to a boil, scraping up any brown bits from the bottom of the pan. Stir in the chicken broth, cream, and chopped tarragon. Boil the sauce until slightly thickened, about 5 minutes.

5) Return the mushrooms to the skillet and cook, stirring once or twice, until heated through, about 1 minute. Pour the mushroom sauce over the chicken breasts and garnish with the tarragon sprigs.

Herbed Chicken with Potatoes and Tomatoes

*A*s colorful as it is flavorful, this dish is sure to please the cook with its simple preparation.

Makes 4 servings

1 (3½-pound) chicken, cut into
  8 pieces
1 teaspoon salt
½ teaspoon sweet Hungarian
  paprika
¼ teaspoon pepper
1 tablespoon olive oil
1 large onion, chopped (about
  1 cup)
2 large garlic cloves, minced
4 medium boiling potatoes, such
  as White Rose (about
  1¼ pounds), scrubbed and cut
  into slices about ½ inch thick

1 cup chicken broth
½ cup dry white wine
1 tablespoon chopped fresh
  thyme or 1 teaspoon dried
1½ teaspoons chopped fresh
  oregano or ½ teaspoon dried
⅛ teaspoon crushed hot red
  pepper
1 (14½-ounce) can diced
  tomatoes, drained
2 bell peppers, preferably 1 red
  and 1 green, cut into ½-inch
  squares

1) Rinse the chicken under cold running water and pat dry. Season with the salt, paprika, and pepper. Heat the olive oil in a 12-inch nonreactive skillet over medium heat. Add the chicken and cook, turning, until nicely browned, about 10 minutes. Remove the chicken and set aside. Pour off and discard all but 1 tablespoon of the oil left in the pan.

2) Add the onion and cook over medium heat, stirring occasionally, until softened but not browned, 3 to 5 minutes. Add the garlic and cook 30 seconds longer. Stir in the potatoes, chicken broth, wine, thyme, oregano, and crushed red pepper. Bring to a boil over medium-high heat, scraping up any brown bits from the bottom of the pan. Return the chicken to the skillet. Reduce the heat to medium-low, cover, and simmer until the potatoes are tender and the chicken is white throughout but still juicy, 20 to 30 minutes.

3) Using a slotted spoon, transfer the chicken and vegetables to a warm serving platter. Cover loosely with foil to keep warm. Add the tomatoes and bell peppers to the skillet and cook over medium-high heat, stirring occasionally, until the peppers are crisp-tender and most of the liquid from the tomatoes has evaporated, 5 to 7 minutes. Pour the mixture over the chicken and serve at once.

Chicken with Raspberry Vinegar and Root Vegetables

A few years back raspberry vinegar was the favored ingredient of the food world and was splashed on just about anything. It takes a recipe like this to remind us of its delicate yet intense flavor. Bring a little taste of summer to your winter meal.

Makes 4 servings

1 (3½-pound) chicken, cut into
  8 pieces
1 teaspoon salt
½ teaspoon pepper
2 tablespoons olive oil
½ cup chicken broth
1 pound red potatoes, cut into
  1-inch chunks
1 pound carrots (5 or 6), cut into
  diagonal slices about ½ inch
  thick

12 shallots, cut in half lengthwise
¾ cup dry white wine
¾ cup raspberry vinegar
3 tablespoons cold butter, cut
  into 3 pieces
1½ tablespoons chopped fresh
  mint or parsley

1) Rinse the chicken under cold running water and pat dry. Season with the salt and pepper. In a 12-inch nonreactive skillet, heat the olive oil over medium heat. Add the chicken and cook, turning, until nicely browned, about 10 minutes. Remove the chicken and set aside. Drain off all the fat from the pan.

2) Add the chicken broth to the skillet and bring to a boil, scraping up any brown bits from the bottom of the pan. Return the chicken to the skillet. Add the potatoes, carrots, and shallots and bring to a boil. Reduce the heat to medium-low, cover, and cook until the vegetables are tender and the chicken is white throughout but still juicy, 20 to 30 minutes. Transfer the chicken and vegetables to a warm serving platter.

3) Add the wine and vinegar to the pan and bring to a boil over high heat. Cook until the sauce is reduced to ¾ cup, 2 to 3 minutes. Remove the pan from the heat. Add the butter and stir until it is melted and smooth. Season with additional salt and pepper to taste. Spoon the sauce over the chicken and vegetables and garnish with the mint.

Chicken with Saffron Rice and Peas

This saffron-scented rice gets an unexpected kick from jalapeño pepper. If saffron is not in your budget, substitute ground turmeric. **Makes 4 servings**

1 (3½-pound) chicken, cut into 8 pieces
1 teaspoon salt
½ teaspoon paprika
½ teaspoon pepper
2 tablespoons olive oil
2 tablespoons butter
1 medium onion, chopped
1 medium red or green bell pepper, cut into ½-inch squares
1 jalapeño or serrano pepper, seeded and minced

2 garlic cloves, minced
⅛ teaspoon ground saffron or 2 large pinches of saffron threads, or ⅛ teaspoon ground turmeric
2 cups chicken broth
1 (14½-ounce) can diced tomatoes, drained
1 cup long-grain white rice
1 (10-ounce) package frozen peas, thawed

1) Rinse the chicken under cold running water and pat dry. Season with the salt, paprika, and pepper. In a 12-inch nonreactive skillet, heat the olive oil over medium heat. Add the chicken and cook, turning, until nicely browned, about 10 minutes. Remove the chicken and set aside.

2) Pour off and discard the oil left in the pan. Add the butter to the skillet and melt over medium heat. Add the onion, bell pepper, jalapeño pepper, and garlic. Cook, stirring occasionally, until softened but not browned, 3 to 5 minutes. Stir in the saffron.

3) Add the chicken broth and bring to a boil over medium-high heat, scraping up any brown bits from the bottom of the pan. Stir in the tomatoes and rice. Return the chicken to the skillet and bring to a boil. Reduce the heat to medium-low, cover, and simmer 15 minutes. Scatter the peas over the top, covered, until the peas are heated through, the rice is tender, and the chicken is white throughout but still juicy, 5 to 15 minutes longer.

Skillet Spaghetti with Ground Chicken

*A*s you might imagine, breaking up strands of uncooked spaghetti can be a real test of dexterity . . . especially when you try to pick them up from the floor. The most efficient method I've found is to put the spaghetti in a plastic bag and go at it.

Makes 4 servings

1 tablespoon olive oil
1 pound ground chicken
1 medium onion, chopped
1 small green bell pepper, chopped
1 garlic clove, minced
½ teaspoon salt
4 ounces thin spaghetti, broken into 1- or 2-inch lengths (1½ to 2 cups)
1 (28-ounce) can diced tomatoes, juices reserved

1 (15-ounce) can tomato sauce
3 tablespoons dry red or white wine
1 tablespoon chopped fresh oregano or 1 teaspoon dried
⅛ teaspoon crushed hot red pepper
2 tablespoons chopped parsley
Grated Parmesan cheese

1) In a 12-inch nonreactive skillet, heat the olive oil over medium heat. Add the chicken, onion, bell pepper, garlic, and salt and cook, stirring occasionally to break up the meat, until the chicken has lost all trace of pink and the vegetables are softened, about 7 minutes.

2) Add the spaghetti and stir to coat. Stir in the tomatoes with their juices, the tomato sauce, wine, oregano, and hot pepper. Bring to a boil, reduce the heat to low, cover, and simmer until the spaghetti is tender but still firm, about 20 minutes. Stir in the parsley. Pass the Parmesan cheese at the table.

Mellow Yellow Chicken
with Vegetables

The yellow color comes from the liberal use of turmeric and curry powder, but the mellow flavor comes from the slow, moist cooking. ***Makes 4 servings***

1 (3½-pound) chicken, cut into 8 pieces
1 teaspoon salt
½ teaspoon ground turmeric
2 tablespoons vegetable oil
1 large onion, halved and cut into slices ½ inch thick
1 red or green bell pepper, cut into ½-inch squares
1 celery rib, cut into diagonal slices about ¼ inch thick
1 carrot, cut into diagonal slices about ¼ inch thick
1 large garlic clove, minced

1 jalapeño or serrano pepper, seeded and minced
1½ teaspoons flour
1½ teaspoons curry powder
¼ teaspoon ground ginger
⅛ teaspoon ground cinnamon
⅛ teaspoon ground cloves
2 medium tomatoes, peeled, seeded, and coarsely chopped
1 cup chicken broth
⅓ cup golden raisins
2 tablespoons coarsely chopped cilantro

1) Rinse the chicken and pat dry. Season with the salt and turmeric. In a large skillet, heat the oil over medium heat. Add the chicken and cook, turning, until browned, about 10 minutes. Remove the chicken and set aside.

2) Drain off all but 2 tablespoons of the fat from the pan. Add the onion, bell pepper, celery, carrot, garlic, and jalapeño pepper. Cook over medium heat, stirring occasionally, until softened but not browned, 3 to 5 minutes. Add the flour, curry powder, ginger, cinnamon, and cloves and cook, stirring, 1 minute longer. Add the tomatoes, chicken broth, and raisins. Bring to a boil over medium-high heat, scraping up any brown bits from the bottom of the pan.

3) Return the chicken to the skillet and bring to a boil. Reduce the heat to medium-low, cover, and simmer until the chicken is white throughout but still juicy, 20 to 30 minutes. Garnish with the chopped cilantro.

Chicken Scaloppine

*C*hicken can be a great substitute
for veal. Serve this light entrée with a butter lettuce salad and plenty
of hot rice or orzo (rice-shaped pasta).   ***Makes 4 servings***

4 skinless, boneless chicken
   breast halves (about
   1½ pounds)
½ teaspoon salt
⅛ teaspoon pepper
2 tablespoons butter

1 tablespoon olive oil
½ cup dry white wine
½ cup chicken broth
3 tablespoons fresh lemon juice
2 tablespoons drained capers
2 tablespoons chopped parsley

1) Rinse the chicken under cold running water and pat dry. Pound the
chicken breasts between 2 sheets of wax paper until flattened evenly to a
¼-inch thickness. Season with the salt and pepper.

2) In a 10-inch nonreactive skillet, melt the butter in the olive oil over
medium heat. Add the chicken and cook, turning once, until white throughout
but still juicy, 4 to 6 minutes. Remove to a warm serving platter.

3) Pour the wine into the pan. Add the chicken broth and bring to a boil
over medium-high heat, scraping up any browned bits from the bottom of the
pan. Cook until the liquid has reduced by half, about 2 minutes. Stir in the
lemon juice, capers, and parsley. Pour the sauce over the chicken and serve at
once.

Indian-Spiced Chicken in Yogurt Sauce

Makes 4 to 6 servings

1½ tablespoons butter or
   vegetable oil
1 small onion, chopped
1 tablespoon grated fresh ginger
3 garlic cloves, minced
1 jalapeño or serrano pepper,
   seeded and minced
1 teaspoon curry powder
½ teaspoon ground cumin
¼ teaspoon ground coriander
⅛ teaspoon cinnamon
Dash of ground cloves

Dash of cayenne
6 skinless, boneless chicken
   breast halves (about
   2¼ pounds)
1 teaspoon salt
¾ cup chicken broth
1 (10-ounce) package frozen peas,
   thawed
¾ cup plain yogurt
Cilantro springs and lemon
   wedges

1) In a large skillet, melt the butter over medium heat. Add the onion, ginger, garlic, and jalapeño pepper and cook, stirring occasionally, until softened but not browned, 3 to 5 minutes. Add the curry powder, cumin, coriander, cinnamon, cloves, and cayenne and cook, stirring, 1 minute longer.

2) Rinse the chicken under cold running water and pat dry. Cut the chicken into ¾-inch pieces and season with the salt. Arrange the chicken pieces in a single layer on top of the onion mixture in the skillet. Add the chicken broth and bring to a simmer over medium heat. Reduce the heat to low, cover, and cook 5 minutes. Turn the chicken pieces over and add the peas. Cover and cook until the peas are heated through and the chicken is white throughout but still juicy, 3 to 5 minutes longer. Using a slotted spoon, transfer the chicken and vegetables to a warm serving platter.

3) Increase the heat to high and boil the liquid until it is thickened and reduced to about 1 tablespoon, 2 to 3 minutes. Remove the skillet from the heat and whisk in the yogurt until well blended. Pour the yogurt sauce over the chicken and vegetables. Garnish with the cilantro sprigs and lemon wedges.

Chicken in a Wok

I t has only taken us a couple of centuries to figure out what the Asians have known all along: woks are a great way to cook. The bowl-like shape of the wok makes it easy to turn out a fresh and healthy meal in record time. The sloped sides of the pan radiate heat, and that is where the cooking process actually takes place. Inexpensive and energy efficient, requiring little maintenance, in other words, just plain practical, woks are essential for any well-supplied kitchen. You can substitute a large skillet, but you'll find that your cooking requires more fat and takes longer.

Round-bottomed woks are made for gas burners. They come with a ring stand to stabilize the wok and keep it from wobbling. When you're ready to start cooking, simply lift off the metal grate from the burner and replace it with the ring to support the wok. Flat-bottomed woks are meant to be placed directly on the heating elements of electric ranges.

Woks can be made from just about any metal, but the economical carbon steel classic still works the best. It responds rapidly to heat adjustments and can be seasoned to build up a relatively nonstick surface. There are even electric woks, which may sound convenient, but don't really get as hot as you need for good stir-frying.

Check Asian markets and import or department stores for the best price on a 14-inch spun carbon steel wok with a single wooden handle. Season and clean as the manufacturer directs, treating the wok as you would a favored cast-iron skillet.

The most efficient way to use this handy utensil is for stir-frying, and here success is all in the timing. Stir-frying is generally done over high heat, using a constant stirring and tossing motion. Ingredients are often added in rapid succession as you toss. Before cooking, everything should be cut and measured and any sauces mixed. In stir-frying, it is generally best that the chicken and vegetables be cut into uniform-size pieces for even cooking. For the sake of organization, I find it very helpful to place a tray near the stove on which I line up the prepared ingredients in the order in which they will be used.

Woks are not just for Chinese cooking, however. In this chapter, you can spice up your life with Cajun-Style Chicken and Rice and Stir-Fried Fajitas. Take your wok on the wild side with Mango Magic and treat your family to Mu Shu Chicken Burritos. This fast and healthy way to cook will become a new way of life in your family.

Crunchy Almond Chicken with Green Beans and Mushrooms

Instead of cutting up whole chicken breasts, save preparation time by purchasing chicken tenders.

Makes 4 to 6 servings

½ cup slivered almonds
4 skinless, boneless chicken
   breast halves (about
   1½ pounds)
¼ cup chicken broth
1 tablespoon soy sauce
2 teaspoons cornstarch
2½ tablespoons peanut or
   vegetable oil
½ teaspoon coarse (kosher) salt

2 celery ribs, cut diagonally into
   slices ¼ inch thick (about
   1 cup)
¼ pound fresh green beans,
   trimmed and cut into 1-inch
   lengths (about 1 cup)
1 cup sliced mushrooms (about
   2 ounces)
¼ teaspoon Asian sesame oil
Dash of hot chili oil or cayenne

1) In a dry wok or large skillet, toast the almonds over medium heat, stirring constantly, until lightly browned, 3 to 4 minutes. Remove the almonds from the pan and set aside to cool.

2) Rinse the chicken under cold running water and pat dry. Cut into strips about 1½ inches long and ½ inch wide. In a small bowl, combine the chicken broth, soy sauce, and cornstarch. Stir until well blended. Set the sauce aside.

3) Heat 1½ tablespoons of the peanut oil in the wok over high heat. Add the chicken and salt and stir-fry until the chicken is white throughout but still juicy, 3 to 5 minutes. Remove the chicken from the wok and set aside.

4) Reduce the heat to medium-high and add the remaining 1 tablespoon peanut oil to the pan. When the oil is hot, add the celery, green beans, and mushrooms and stir-fry until the vegetables are crisp-tender, 1 to 2 minutes.

5) Stir in the reserved chicken and sauce and boil until the liquid is slightly thickened, 1 to 2 minutes longer. Add the almonds, sesame oil, and chili oil, toss, and serve at once.

Spicy Chicken with Sweet Basil

As shown in this recipe, sweet basil is often treated as a vegetable in Thai cooking. Take care when stir-frying crushed red pepper—the fumes are very potent. And be sure to make lots of rice to cool the delicious fire of the finished dish.

Makes 4 servings

3 skinless boneless chicken breast halves (about 1 pound)
2 tablespoons peanut or vegetable oil
4 garlic cloves, minced
½ to 1 teaspoon crushed hot red pepper
4 to 6 jalapeño or serrano peppers, seeded and coarsely chopped

3 tablespoons Thai fish sauce (nam pla)* or soy sauce
½ teaspoon sugar
1 cup (loosely packed) small fresh basil leaves
2 scallions, thinly sliced
Lime wedges

1) Rinse the chicken under cold running water and pat dry. Cut into thin strips.

2) In a wok or large skillet, heat the peanut oil over medium-high heat. Add the garlic and crushed red pepper and cook, stirring, until fragrant, about 30 seconds.

3) Add the chicken and stir-fry until white throughout but still juicy, 3 to 5 minutes. Add the jalapeño peppers, fish sauce, and sugar and stir-fry until the peppers begin to soften, about 2 minutes. Stir in the basil and serve at once. Sprinkle the scallions on top and garnish with the lime wedges.

*Available at Asian markets and in the Asian foods section of many supermarkets.

Mu Shu Chicken Burritos

F*lour tortillas make a handy substitute for the thin Mandarin pancakes served in Chinese restaurants. Look for jars of hoisin sauce in the Asian foods section of most supermarkets.*

Makes 2 to 4 servings

2 skinless, boneless chicken
  breast halves (about ¾ pound)
3 tablespoons soy sauce
1 tablespoon cornstarch
1 teaspoon grated fresh ginger
⅛ teaspoon crushed hot red
  pepper
2 tablespoons peanut or vegetable
  oil
2 cups finely shredded Napa or
  other green cabbage
¼ pound mushrooms, thinly
  sliced

1 small carrot, peeled and
  coarsely shredded
2 scallions, thinly sliced
1 egg, beaten
2 tablespoons dry vermouth or
  sherry
½ teaspoon sugar
½ teaspoon Asian sesame oil
3 tablespoons hoisin sauce
4 (6½- or 7-inch) flour tortillas,
  warmed
¼ cup coarsely chopped cilantro

1) Rinse the chicken under cold running water and pat dry. Cut into strips about ¼ inch thick. In a medium bowl or a heavy-duty 1-quart plastic food storage bag, combine the chicken with 1 tablespoon of the soy sauce, the cornstarch, ginger, and hot pepper. Cover and marinate 15 minutes at room temperature.

2) In a wok or large skillet, heat the peanut oil over high heat. Add the chicken mixture and stir-fry until the chicken is white throughout but still juicy, about 3 minutes.

3) Add the cabbage, mushrooms, carrot, and scallions and stir-fry until the vegetables are softened, about 2 minutes. Add the egg and stir-fry until the egg is softly scrambled, about 1 minute.

4) Add the remaining 2 tablespoons soy sauce, the vermouth, sugar, sesame oil, and 1 tablespoon of the hoisin sauce to the wok. Stir-fry until the ingredients are well coated, about 1 minute.

5) Brush the centers of the warmed tortillas with the remaining 2 tablespoons hoisin sauce. Spoon the chicken mixture down the center of each tortilla and sprinkle with 1 tablespoon cilantro. Fold in both sides of the tortillas. Fold the bottom quarters of tortilla up over the filling, then roll up the tortillas to enclose. Serve with additional hoisin sauce for dipping, if desired.

Flash-in-the-Pan Winter Stir-Fry

Even during the most dismal *months for produce, it's still easy to make a healthy and attractive chicken dinner in minutes.*

Makes 4 servings

3 skinless, boneless chicken
   breast halves (about 1 pound)
1 tablespoon peanut or vegetable
   oil
¼ teaspoon coarse (kosher) salt
2 teaspoons grated fresh ginger
1 garlic clove, minced
2 pounds bok choy or Napa
   cabbage, cut into slices about
   ¼ inch thick (about 6 cups)

1 medium onion, cut into wedges
   about ¼ inch thick
6 scallions, cut diagonally into
   1½-inch lengths
3 tablespoons soy sauce

1) Rinse the chicken under cold running water and pat dry. Cut into ¾-inch pieces.

2) In a wok or large skillet, heat the peanut oil and salt over medium-high heat. Add the ginger and garlic and stir-fry until fragrant, about 30 seconds. Add the chicken and cook, stirring frequently, until white throughout but still juicy, 3 to 4 minutes. Add the bok choy, onion, and scallions and stir-fry until crisp-tender, 2 to 3 minutes. Add the soy sauce and cook, stirring, 1 minute longer.

Chicken with Broccoli and Cashews

This popular combination of *flavors works well with rice.*

Makes 4 to 6 servings

4 skinless, boneless chicken
   breast halves (about
   1½ pounds)
½ cup chicken broth
3 tablespoons soy sauce
2 teaspoons cornstarch
½ teaspoon sugar
2 tablespoons peanut or vegetable
   oil
¼ teaspoon coarse (kosher) salt

1 teaspoon grated fresh ginger
1 garlic clove, minced
1 bunch of broccoli (about 1
   pound), cut into florets and
   ½-inch pieces (about 3 cups)
1 (8-ounce) can sliced water
   chestnuts, drained
Pinch of crushed hot red pepper
1 cup unsalted cashews

1) Rinse the chicken under cold running water and pat dry. Cut into
¾-inch pieces.

2) In a small bowl, combine the chicken broth, soy sauce, cornstarch, and
sugar. Stir until well blended.

3) In a wok or large skillet, heat 1 tablespoon of the peanut oil and the salt
over high heat. Add the ginger and garlic and cook, stirring, until fragrant,
about 30 seconds. Add the chicken and stir-fry until white throughout but still
juicy, 3 to 4 minutes. Remove the chicken mixture from the wok and set aside.

4) Heat the remaining 1 tablespoon peanut oil over high heat. Add the
broccoli and stir-fry until crisp-tender, 2 to 3 minutes. Add the chicken broth
mixture, water chestnuts, and hot pepper and cook, stirring frequently, until the
sauce is slightly thickened, 2 to 3 minutes. Add the cashews and stir-fry
1 minute longer.

Cajun-Style Chicken and Rice

High in flavor and low in cost, *this "dirty rice" is perfect for a casual meal.* ***Makes 4 servings***

3 tablespoons peanut or vegetable oil
3 tablespoons flour
1 large onion, finely chopped
3 medium celery ribs, finely chopped
1 small green bell pepper, finely chopped
4 garlic cloves, minced
1 pound ground chicken
½ pound chicken livers and/or gizzards, finely chopped

1 teaspoon salt
¼ teaspoon cayenne
¼ teaspoon pepper
¼ teaspoon ground cumin
¼ teaspoon dried oregano
¼ teaspoon dried thyme leaves
Dash of hot pepper sauce
1½ cups chicken broth
4 to 5 cups cooked long-grain white rice
3 scallions, coarsely chopped

1) In a wok, heat the peanut oil over high heat. Stir in the flour and reduce the heat to medium. Cook, stirring constantly, until the mixture turns dark brown without burning, 3 to 5 minutes. Add the onion, celery, bell pepper, and garlic and stir-fry until the vegetables are softened but not browned, 2 to 3 minutes.

2) Increase the heat to high and stir in the ground chicken and chicken livers. Stir-fry until the ground chicken has lost all trace of pink, about 7 minutes. Stir in the salt, cayenne, pepper, cumin, oregano, thyme, and hot pepper sauce.

3) Add the chicken broth and bring to a boil, stirring and scraping up any brown bits from the bottom of the pan. Add the rice and cook, stirring often, until heated through, 2 to 3 minutes. Sprinkle the scallions on top and serve.

Chutney Chicken Stir-Fry

This sweet-sounding chicken
packs a bit of a wallop, so you may want to serve it with either rice
or couscous. You'll also notice that the unusual addition of butter
brings an unexpected and very pleasant richness to this cross-
cultural dish. *Makes 4 servings*

3 skinless, boneless chicken
  breast halves (about 1 pound)
¾ cup mango chutney, finely
  chopped
½ cup chicken broth
3 tablespoons Japanese white rice
  wine vinegar
2 tablespoons unsalted butter
2 tablespoons peanut or vegetable
  oil

2 tablespoons grated fresh ginger
1 large garlic clove, minced
¼ teaspoon coarse (kosher) salt
¼ teaspoon crushed hot red
  pepper
2 scallions, thinly sliced
2 tablespoons coarsely chopped
  peanuts

1) Rinse the chicken under cold running water and pat dry. Cut into
¾-inch pieces.

2) In a small bowl, combine the chutney, chicken broth, and vinegar.

3) In a wok or large skillet, melt the butter in the oil over medium-high
heat. Add the ginger, garlic, and salt and stir-fry until just fragrant, about 30
seconds. Add the chicken and hot pepper and stir-fry until the chicken is white
throughout but still juicy, 3 to 4 minutes. Remove the chicken mixture and set
aside.

4) Add the chutney mixture to the wok and bring to a boil over medium-
high heat. Cook, stirring occasionally, until slightly thickened, 2 to 3 minutes.
Return the chicken to the wok and stir-fry 1 minute longer. Remove the chicken
mixture to a warm platter. Sprinkle the scallions and peanuts on top and serve.

Taipei Curry-in-a-Hurry

If you have access to an ethnic market or specialty shop that sells jars of Thai or Indian curry paste, by all means use it. Otherwise good-quality Madras curry powder will do. Serve this with lots of rice and maybe a cool salad of cucumbers and yogurt. **Makes 4 servings**

3 skinless, boneless chicken breast halves (about 1 pound)
2 tablespoons peanut or vegetable oil
1 medium onion, cut into wedges about ¼ inch thick
2 garlic cloves, minced
1 teaspoon grated fresh ginger
¼ teaspoon coarse (kosher) salt
1 tablespoon curry paste or curry powder, or to taste

1½ cups chicken broth
1½ tablespoons soy sauce
2 medium red or other boiling potatoes (about 1 pound), cut into ¾-inch cubes
3 medium carrots (about ½ pound), peeled and cut into quarters lengthwise, then into sticks 2 inches long by ¼ inch thick

1) Rinse the chicken under cold running water and pat dry. Cut into ¾-inch pieces.

2) In a wok or large skillet, heat the peanut oil over high heat. Add the onion, garlic, ginger, and salt and stir-fry until just fragrant, 1 to 2 minutes. Add the chicken and cook, stirring frequently, until white throughout but still juicy, 3 to 4 minutes. Remove the chicken mixture and set aside.

3) Add the curry paste, chicken broth, soy sauce, potatoes, and carrots to the wok. Bring to a simmer over medium-high heat, stirring constantly. Reduce the heat to medium, cover, and simmer 10 minutes. Stir in the chicken mixture and cook, uncovered, stirring occasionally, until the vegetables are tender and the sauce is slightly thickened, 8 to 10 minutes longer.

Stir-Fried Fajitas

You don't always have to fire up
the outdoor grill to enjoy fajitas—here's a quick and easy way to
make great ones in your kitchen. Substitute chicken tenders for the
breast halves to cut your preparation time even further.

Makes 6 servings

6 skinless, boneless chicken
   breast halves (about
   2¼ pounds)
3 tablespoons lime juice
3 tablespoons vegetable oil
2 or 3 garlic cloves, minced
1 teaspoon salt
½ teaspoon ground cumin
⅛ teaspoon cayenne
1 large onion, halved and cut into
   slices ¼ inch thick

1 large red bell pepper, cut into
   strips about ¼ inch thick
12 warm flour tortillas or 6 halved
   warm pita breads
Guacamole or diced avocado
Salsa or diced tomatoes
Shredded lettuce or cilantro sprigs
Shredded Monterey Jack and/or
   Cheddar cheese
Pickled jalapeño peppers
Sour cream

1) Rinse the chicken under cold running water and pat dry. Cut into strips
about ¼ inch thick. In a medium bowl or heavy-duty 1-gallon plastic food
storage bag, combine the chicken, lime juice, 1 tablespoon of the oil, the garlic,
salt, cumin, and cayenne. Cover and marinate at room temperature at least
15 minutes or as long as 2 hours.

2) In a wok or large skillet, heat 1 tablespoon of the oil over high heat. Add
the chicken, in batches if necessary, and stir-fry until the chicken is lightly
browned outside and white throughout but still juicy, 3 to 5 minutes per batch.
Remove the chicken and set aside.

3) Add the remaining 1 tablespoon oil to the wok and heat over high heat.
Add the onion and bell pepper and stir-fry until crisp-tender, 3 to 5 minutes.
Return the chicken to the wok and stir-fry until heated through, about 1 minute.
Transfer the chicken mixture to a warm serving platter. Serve with a basket of
warm tortillas and pass the remaining ingredients for accompaniments at the
table.

Mango Magic

Although many of us consider the mango an exotic fruit, to over half the world it is better known than the apple. Serve this refreshing stir-fry over hot cooked rice.

Makes 4 servings

4 skinless, boneless chicken
   breast halves (about
   1½ pounds)
2 tablespoons peanut or vegetable
   oil
½ teaspoon coarse (kosher) salt
2 teaspoons grated fresh ginger
1 garlic clove, minced
⅛ teaspoon crushed hot red
   pepper

1 large red bell pepper, cut into
   ½-inch squares
1 medium mango (about
   ¾ pound), peeled, seeded, and
   cut into ½-inch dice
3 scallions, thinly sliced
1 tablespoon soy sauce
⅛ teaspoon sugar

1) Rinse the chicken under cold running water and pat dry. Cut into
¾-inch pieces.

2) In a wok or large skillet, heat 1 tablespoon of the peanut oil and the salt
over high heat. Add the ginger, garlic, and hot pepper and cook, stirring
constantly, until fragrant, about 30 seconds. Add the chicken and stir-fry until
the chicken is white throughout but still juicy, 3 to 4 minutes. Remove the
chicken from the wok and set aside.

3) Heat the remaining 1 tablespoon peanut oil over high heat. Add the bell
pepper and stir-fry until crisp-tender, 2 to 3 minutes. Add the chicken, mango,
scallions, soy sauce, and sugar. Stir-fry until heated through, 2 to 3 minutes.

Chicken with Peas, Pancetta, and Mint

Unsmoked Italian-style bacon, known as pancetta, is available at many delicatessens. Serve this dish over hot rice cooked in chicken broth instead of water.

Makes 4 servings

4 skinless, boneless chicken
  breast halves (about
  1½ pounds)
1 teaspoon salt
¼ teaspoon pepper
2 tablespoons peanut or vegetable
  oil
1 garlic clove, minced
¼ cup chopped pancetta (about
  2 ounces) or 4 bacon slices,
  chopped

1 (10-ounce) package frozen peas,
  thawed
2 scallions, thinly sliced
1 tablespoon chopped fresh mint
  or 1 teaspoon dried
Dash of cayenne
Lemon wedges

1) Rinse the chicken under cold running water and pat dry. Cut into ¾-inch pieces and season with ½ teaspoon of the salt and the pepper.

2) In a wok or large skillet, heat the oil over medium-high heat. Add the garlic and cook until fragrant, about 30 seconds. Add the chicken and pancetta and stir-fry until the chicken is white throughout but still juicy, about 3 minutes.

3) Add the remaining ½ teaspoon salt, the peas, scallions, mint, and cayenne. Stir-fry until heated through, about 2 minutes. Serve with lemon wedges to squeeze over each serving.

Sweet and Sour Stir-Fry

People who routinely view vegetables with contempt usually find this classic dish a welcome exception to their rule.   **Makes 4 to 6 servings**

4 skinless, boneless chicken breast halves (about 1½ pounds)
2 tablespoons red wine vinegar
1 tablespoon cornstarch
1 (20-ounce) can unsweetened pineapple chunks, drained, juices reserved
2 tablespoons brown sugar
2 tablespoons ketchup or tomato paste

2 teaspoons soy sauce
Pinch of crushed hot red pepper
2½ tablespoons peanut or vegetable oil
1 large onion, cut into wedges about ¼ inch thick
1 large green bell pepper, cut into ¾-inch squares
1 teaspoon grated fresh ginger or ¼ teaspoon ground ginger

1) Rinse the chicken under cold running water and pat dry. Cut into ¾-inch pieces.

2) In a small bowl, combine the vinegar, cornstarch, reserved pineapple juices, brown sugar, ketchup, soy sauce, and hot pepper until well blended.

3) In a wok or large skillet, heat 1 tablespoon of the peanut oil over high heat. Add the onion, green pepper, and ginger and stir-fry until the vegetables are crisp-tender, 2 to 3 minutes. Remove the vegetables and set aside.

4) Heat the remaining 1½ tablespoons peanut oil in the wok over high heat. Add the chicken and stir-fry until white throughout but still juicy, 3 to 4 minutes. Stir the vinegar mixture and add to the wok. Cook, stirring constantly, until the sauce turns clear, comes to a boil, and thickens, 1 to 2 minutes.

5) Return the onion mixture to the wok. Stir in the pineapple chunks. Cover and cook until heated through, about 2 minutes longer.

Chicken with Pineapple and Red Bell Pepper

My friend Joyce Jue, an internationally recognized authority on Asian cuisines, makes this dish frequently. When time is at a premium, purchase a spit-roasted chicken from a Chinese market or delicatessen and check your supermarket produce section or salad bar for pre-cut fresh pineapple. Use canned pineapple only as a last resort.

Makes 4 to 6 servings

1 Crispy Roast Chicken (page 148)
¼ cup chicken broth
2 tablespoons brown sugar
2 tablespoons red wine vinegar
1 tablespoon soy sauce
  (preferably dark)
1½ teaspoons grated fresh ginger
1 tablespoon peanut or vegetable
  oil

½ teaspoon coarse (kosher) salt
1 medium onion, cut into ¾-inch
  squares
1 medium red bell pepper, cut
  into ¾-inch squares
1½ cups cubed (¾-inch) fresh
  pineapple (half a 2-pound
  pineapple)

1) Remove the chicken meat from the bones. Remove the skin, if desired. Cut the chicken meat into strips ¾ inch wide and 2 inches long.

2) In a small bowl, combine the chicken broth, brown sugar, vinegar, soy sauce, and ginger. Stir to mix well. Set the sauce aside.

3) In a wok or large skillet, heat the peanut oil over high heat. Add the onion and bell pepper and stir-fry until the bell pepper is bright red, about 1 minute.

4) Add the sauce and cook, stirring constantly, until well mixed, about 15 seconds. Add the chicken and cook until heated through, about 15 seconds. Add the pineapple and cook, stirring, until just heated through, about 1 minute.

Chicken and Pineapple Stir-Fry

T_his slightly spicy stir-fry is the_
inspired creation of fellow food professional Michelle Schmidt.
Be sure to serve with plenty of hot rice. **_Makes 4 to 6 servings_**

4 skinless, boneless chicken
   breast halves (about
   1½ pounds)
5 tablespoons soy sauce
2 garlic cloves, minced
½ teaspoon salt
1 tablespoon medium-dry sherry,
   dry vermouth, or chicken broth
1 teaspoon cornstarch
2 tablespoons peanut or vegetable
   oil

1 large red bell pepper, cut into
   2¼-inch strips
6 scallions, cut into 2-inch lengths
1½ cups cubed fresh pineapple
   (half of a 2-pound pineapple cut
   into ¾-inch cubes) or 1½ cups
   unsweetened canned pineapple
   chunks, drained
1 teaspoon sugar
⅜ teaspoon crushed hot red
   pepper

1) Rinse the chicken under cold running water and pat dry. Cut into
¾-inch pieces. In a medium bowl or a heavy-duty 1-quart plastic food storage
bag, combine the chicken, 3 tablespoons of the soy sauce, the garlic, and salt.
Let stand 15 minutes at room temperature.

2) In a small bowl, combine the remaining 2 tablespoons soy sauce, the
sherry, and cornstarch and stir until well blended. Set aside.

3) In a wok or large skillet, heat 1 tablespoon of the peanut oil over high
heat. Add the chicken and stir-fry until white throughout but still juicy, 3 to 4
minutes. Remove the chicken and set aside.

4) Add the remaining 1 tablespoon peanut oil to the wok and heat over
high heat. Add the bell pepper and stir-fry until crisp-tender, about 1 to 2
minutes. Add the scallions and stir-fry about 30 seconds.

5) Add the pineapple and sprinkle on the sugar. Stir-fry until some of the
pineapple chunks begin to brown around the edges, about 1 minute. Add
the reserved cornstarch mixture and bring to a boil. Add the chicken and hot
pepper and cook, stirring, until heated through, 1 to 2 minutes longer.

Stir-Fried Chicken with Summer Squash

*T*his combination of green and yellow squash makes an exceptionally lovely presentation. Serve with orzo (rice-shaped pasta) tossed with a bit of extra-virgin olive oil and grated Parmesan cheese. **Makes 4 servings**

4 skinless, boneless chicken breast halves (about 1½ pounds)
1 teaspoon salt
¼ teaspoon pepper
2 tablespoons peanut or vegetable oil
1 garlic clove, minced
2 medium green zucchini, halved lengthwise and thinly sliced

2 medium yellow zucchini or crookneck squash, halved lengthwise and thinly sliced
4 oil-packed sun-dried tomato halves, drained and finely chopped
1 tablespoon chopped fresh rosemary or 1 teaspoon dried

1) Rinse the chicken under cold running water and pat dry. Cut into ¾-inch pieces and season with ½ teaspoon of the salt and the pepper.

2) In a wok or large skillet, heat 1 tablespoon of the peanut oil over medium-high heat. Stir in the garlic and cook until fragrant, about 30 seconds. Add the chicken and stir-fry until white throughout but still juicy, 3 to 4 minutes. Transfer to a plate and set aside.

3) Heat the remaining 1 tablespoon peanut oil in the wok. Add the green and yellow zucchini and stir-fry until crisp-tender, 3 to 5 minutes.

4) Return the chicken to the pan. Add the remaining ½ teaspoon salt, the sun-dried tomatoes, and rosemary and stir-fry until heated through, about 2 minutes. Serve at once.

Thai-Style Chicken Thighs with Peanuts and Mint

Makes 4 to 6 servings

5 skinless, boneless chicken thighs (about 1 pound)
2 tablespoons chicken broth
2 or 3 small red or green jalapeño or serrano peppers, thinly sliced into rings
1 tablespoon Thai fish sauce (nam pla)* or soy sauce
2 teaspoons fresh lime juice
1 teaspoon sugar
2 tablespoons peanut or vegetable oil

1 teaspoon grated fresh ginger
3 garlic cloves, minced
4 shallots, thinly sliced
2 medium carrots, peeled and finely shredded (about 1½ cups)
½ cup loosely packed small fresh basil leaves
3 tablespoons coarsely chopped unsalted peanuts
2 teaspoons coarsely chopped fresh mint
Lime wedges

1) Rinse the chicken under cold running water and pat dry. Cut into ¾-inch pieces. In a small bowl, combine the chicken broth, jalapeño peppers, fish sauce, lime juice, and sugar. Stir until well blended.

2) In a wok or large nonreactive skillet, heat 1 tablespoon of the peanut oil over medium-high heat. Add the ginger and garlic and stir-fry until fragrant, about 30 seconds. Add half of the chicken and shallots and cook, stirring often, until the chicken is almost cooked through, 3 to 4 minutes. Remove the chicken mixture and set aside. Repeat with the remaining 1 tablespoon peanut oil, the chicken, and shallots.

3) Return all the chicken with the shallots to the pan. Stir in the carrots and chicken broth mixture. Cook, stirring often, until the carrots are crisp-tender and the sauce is slightly thickened, 1 to 2 minutes. Stir in the basil and cook until the leaves are just wilted, about 10 seconds. Remove to a warm serving platter. Sprinkle the peanuts and mint on top. Garnish with lime wedges.

Chicken in a Stew Pot

The stew pot, also known as a Dutch oven, is designed for slow cooking over low heat. The deep straight sides of the pot create steam as the food cooks, making it ideal for long-simmering, fuss-free meals. It is important to purchase a heavy-bottomed pan that will withstand high heat for browning without burning, and then withstand a little neglect while your supper gently bubbles and simmers as you pursue other tasks around the house.

The capacity of Dutch ovens ranges from 4 to 14 quarts, with a 5- to 6-quart pot as the standard. When making this somewhat substantial financial invest-ment, it's best to purchase a pot with heatproof handles that can go from stovetop to oven. A heavy enameled cast-iron pot is a lifetime investment in good cooking. Its smooth interior surface is nonreactive to acidic foods, the invisible cast-iron interior is a good conductor of even heat, and it looks good enough to bring directly to the table. There are also some excellent aluminum-based pots covered with stainless steel or other nonstick materials.

The idea of a stew pot may seem old-fashioned, but the recipes in this chapter are not. Enjoy Chicken with Green Beans in Peanut Sauce and savor Spring Chicken Risotto. Make a run for the border with Mexicali Chicken Stew and Chicken Chili Pronto. Satisfy the gypsy in your soul with Chicken Paprikash, and ward off evil vampires with Chicken Thighs with 40 Cloves of Garlic. My favorite recipe, Chicken with Pinot Noir and Wild Mushrooms, can also be found in this chapter.

So relax, light the candles, and play some soft music. You have a chicken in the stew pot and dinner is cooking itself.

Chicken with Green Beans in Peanut Sauce

Jasmine rice is a perfect
accompaniment to this supper with Indonesian overtones.

Makes 4 servings

1 (3½-pound) chicken, cut into
  8 pieces
¾ teaspoon salt
½ teaspoon paprika
2 tablespoons vegetable oil
1 medium onion, chopped
1 garlic clove, minced
⅓ cup smooth or chunky peanut
  butter

⅛ teaspoon cayenne
1 (13½-ounce) can unsweetened
  coconut milk
½ cup chicken broth
1½ tablespoons soy sauce
1½ pounds fresh green beans, cut
  into 1-inch lengths
⅓ cup chopped peanuts

1) Rinse the chicken under cold running water and pat dry. Season with the salt and paprika. In a 4- or 5-quart Dutch oven, heat the oil over medium heat. Add the chicken, in batches if necessary, and cook, turning, until nicely browned, about 10 minutes. Remove the chicken and set aside.

2) Drain all but 1 tablespoon of fat from the pot. Add the onion and garlic to the pot and cook over medium heat, stirring occasionally, until softened but not browned, 3 to 5 minutes. Stir in the peanut butter and cayenne. Gradually whisk in the coconut milk and chicken broth to blend well. Increase the heat to medium-high. Stir in the soy sauce and bring to a boil, scraping up any brown bits from the bottom of the pot.

3) Return the chicken to pot. Reduce the heat to medium-low, cover, and cook 10 minutes. Add the green beans, cover, and cook until the beans are crisp-tender and the chicken is white throughout but still juicy, 10 to 15 minutes longer.

4) Using a slotted spoon, transfer the chicken and green beans to a warm serving platter. Increase the heat to medium-high and boil until the sauce has thickened, 3 to 5 minutes. Pour the sauce over the chicken and green beans and sprinkle the peanuts on top.

Quick Ground Chicken and Black Bean Mole

Moles *are complex Mexican sauces, which often contain chiles, herbs, nuts, and chocolate. This streamlined version provides all the flavor with half the work.*

Makes 4 servings

2 tablespoons hulled pumpkin
  seeds (pepitas)
1 tablespoon vegetable oil
1 pound ground chicken
1 medium onion, chopped
2 garlic cloves, minced
1 teaspoon salt
1 (15-ounce) can black beans,
  rinsed and drained
1 (14½-ounce) can stewed
  tomatoes
1 (8-ounce) can tomato sauce

2 tablespoons raisins
1 tablespoon dark brown sugar
1 tablespoon unsweetened cocoa
  powder
1 teaspoon chili powder
1 teaspoon ground cumin
½ teaspoon dried oregano
¼ teaspoon crushed hot red
  pepper
Warm flour tortillas and sour
  cream

1) In a 4- to 5-quart Dutch oven, toast the pumpkin seeds over medium heat, stirring often, until they pop around in the pot and begin to brown, 3 to 4 minutes. Remove the seeds and set aside to cool.

2) In the same pot, heat the oil over medium-high heat. Add the chicken, onion, garlic, and salt and cook, stirring occasionally to break up the meat, until the chicken has lost all trace of pink and the onion has softened, about 7 minutes.

3) Stir in the beans, stewed tomatoes, tomato sauce, pumpkin seeds, raisins, brown sugar, cocoa, chili powder, cumin, oregano, and crushed red pepper. Bring to a boil. Reduce the heat to low, cover, and cook, stirring occasionally, 30 minutes. Serve with tortillas and pass the sour cream at the table.

Soft Tostadas with White Chili

Who says chili has to have a red sauce? I like to serve this quick and elegant rendition over mixed salad greens on warm tortillas. **Makes 4 servings**

5 skinless, boneless chicken
   thighs (about 1 pound)
1 teaspoon salt
2 tablespoons vegetable oil
1 medium onion, chopped
2 or 3 jalapeño or serrano
   peppers, seeded and minced
3 garlic cloves, minced
1 teaspoon ground cumin
½ teaspoon dried oregano
⅛ teaspoon cayenne
1 cup chicken broth

1 (15-ounce) can Great Northern
   (large white) beans, rinsed and
   drained
1 (12-ounce) can tomatillos,
   drained and chopped
¼ cup coarsely chopped cilantro
4 (6½- or 7-inch) corn or flour
   tortillas
4 cups mixed tender lettuce
   leaves or watercress
½ cup shredded Monterey Jack
   cheese (about 2 ounces)

1) Rinse the chicken under cold running water and pat dry. Cut into ¾-inch pieces and season with ½ teaspoon of the salt.

2) In a 4- or 5-quart Dutch oven, heat 1 tablespoon of the oil over medium-high heat. Add the chicken and cook, turning, until lightly browned, about 5 minutes. Remove the chicken and set aside.

3) Heat the remaining 1 tablespoon oil in the same pot over medium heat. Add the onion, jalapeño peppers, garlic, cumin, oregano, and cayenne and cook, stirring occasionally, until the onion is softened but not browned, 3 to 5 minutes. Stir in the chicken broth and bring to a boil.

4) Reduce the heat to low and stir in the chicken, the remaining ½ teaspoon salt, the beans, and tomatillos. Cook, uncovered, stirring occasionally, until the sauce has thickened slightly, 20 to 25 minutes.

5) Just before serving, stir in the cilantro. Place a warm tortilla on each of 4 plates. Top each tortilla with 1 cup of the greens, a generous serving of the white chili, and 2 tablespoons of the cheese.

Chicken Chili Pronto

*T*o create a Texas favorite, pour *piping hot chili over corn chips and top with minced onion, sliced pickled jalapeño peppers, and shredded Cheddar cheese.*

Makes 4 servings

1 tablespoon vegetable oil
1 pound ground chicken
1 medium onion, chopped
3 garlic cloves, minced
2 tablespoons chili powder
1 teaspoon salt
½ teaspoon ground cumin

⅛ teaspoon cayenne
1 (28-ounce) can crushed
  tomatoes with added puree
1 (15-ounce) can pinto or kidney
  beans, rinsed and drained
1 (4-ounce) can diced green
  chiles

1) In a 4- or 5-quart Dutch oven, heat the oil over medium-high heat. Add the chicken, onion, garlic, chili powder, salt, cumin, and cayenne and cook, stirring to break up the meat, until the chicken has lost all trace of pink and the onion has softened, about 7 minutes.

2) Stir in the tomatoes with their puree, the beans, and the chiles with their juices and bring to a boil. Reduce the heat to low and cook, stirring occasionally, 15 minutes.

Chicken Thighs with 40 Cloves of Garlic

My friend Lonnie renamed this dish "Mid-Life Chicken—40 Cloves of Garlic for Those Thighs." No matter what you call it, this supper is both delicious and a snap to make—especially if your produce market sells jars of peeled whole garlic cloves.   **Makes 4 to 6 servings**

10 chicken thighs on the bone
   (about 2½ pounds)
1½ teaspoons salt
1 teaspoon paprika
½ teaspoon pepper
2 tablespoons olive oil
18 small red potatoes (about
   1½ pounds), cut in half

40 garlic cloves, peeled (about
   3 heads)
2 medium celery ribs, chopped
1 tablespoon chopped fresh
   rosemary or 1 teaspoon dried
½ cup dry white wine
Crusty French bread, sliced

1) Preheat the oven to 375 degrees F. Rinse the chicken under cold running water and pat dry. Season with 1 teaspoon of the salt, the paprika, and pepper.

2) In a 5-quart ovenproof Dutch oven or flameproof casserole, heat the olive oil over medium-high heat. Add the chicken, in batches if necessary, and cook, turning, until nicely browned, about 10 minutes. Remove the pot from the heat. Remove the chicken thighs and set aside. Drain off and discard all but 1 tablespoon of fat from the pot.

3) Add the remaining ½ teaspoon salt, the potatoes, garlic, celery, and rosemary to the pot. Arrange the chicken thighs on top, skin side up. Pour the wine over the chicken. Cover and bake until the chicken is white throughout but still juicy and the potatoes are tender, about 1½ hours. Serve directly from the pot or remove the chicken to a warm serving platter and surround with the vegetables. Spread the butter-soft garlic cloves onto the French bread slices.

Chicken and Wild Mushroom Stew with Scallion Dumplings

If wild mushrooms are not available, cultivated ones will make an equally delicious though less exotic stew. **Makes 4 to 6 servings**

1 (3½-pound) chicken, cut into
   8 pieces
¼ cup flour
1½ teaspoons salt
½ teaspoon pepper
½ teaspoon paprika
2 tablespoons olive oil
½ pound fresh shiitake or other
   wild mushrooms, cut into halves
   or quarters
2 large shallots, finely chopped
4 cups chicken broth
9 small red potatoes (about
   ¾ pound), scrubbed and cut in
   half

3 medium carrots, peeled and cut
   diagonally into slices about
   ¼ inch thick
1 medium celery rib, chopped
1 (9-ounce) package frozen Italian
   green beans, thawed
2 teaspoons chopped fresh thyme
   or ½ teaspoon dried
3 tablespoons chopped parsley
2 cups buttermilk baking mix,
   such as Bisquick
¾ cup milk
1 large scallion, finely chopped

1) Rinse the chicken under cold running water and pat dry. Mix the flour, 1 teaspoon of the salt, the pepper, and paprika in a paper bag. Add the chicken to the bag, a few pieces at a time, and shake until well coated. Shake off the excess seasoned flour.

2) In a 5-quart Dutch oven, heat the olive oil over medium-high heat. Add the chicken, in batches if necessary, and cook, turning, until nicely browned, about 10 minutes per batch. Remove the chicken and set aside.

3) Reduce the heat to medium. Add the mushrooms and shallots to the pot and cook, stirring often, until the mushrooms give up their juices and the liquid evaporates, 5 to 7 minutes. Drain off and discard any fat left in the pot.

4) Add the remaining ½ teaspoon salt, the chicken broth, potatoes, carrots, and celery. Bring to a boil, scraping up any brown bits from the bottom of the pot. Return the chicken to the pot and bring to a boil. Reduce the heat to low, cover, and cook until the chicken is white throughout but still juicy, 20 to 30 minutes.

5) Skim off and discard any fat from the top of the cooking liquid. Stir in the green beans, thyme, and parsley. Reduce the heat to medium-low.

6) In a medium bowl, combine the baking mix and milk. Blend just until evenly moistened. Stir in the scallions. Using 2 large spoons, shape about 2 tablespoons of dough at a time into rounded dumplings and gently scoop onto the top of the stew, preferably on top of a piece of chicken. Allow about 1 inch between each dumpling. Cover the pan tightly and cook, without lifting the cover, until the dumplings are puffed and firm to the touch, about 20 minutes.

Chicken with Pinot Noir and Wild Mushrooms

Here's a variation on the classic
*Coq au Vin—easy to make and sure to satisfy. The sauce is so
intense and flavorful, no one will guess you used canned broth.
Crusty bread and a salad of bitter greens round out the meal.*

Makes 4 servings

4 thick bacon slices, cut into
½-inch pieces
20 small white (pearl) onions,
peeled
⅛ teaspoon sugar
1 tablespoon plus 1 teaspoon
unsalted butter
½ pound fresh wild mushrooms,
such as chanterelles or
shiitakes, cut into halves or
quarters
1 (3½-pound) chicken, cut into
8 pieces

¼ cup plus 2 teaspoons flour
¾ teaspoon salt
½ teaspoon pepper
1 tablespoon vegetable or olive oil
1 tablespoon Dijon mustard
1 tablespoon tomato paste
1 (14½-ounce) can beef broth
1 cup Pinot Noir or other dry red
wine
¾ teaspoon chopped fresh thyme
or ¼ teaspoon dried
2 tablespoons chopped parsley

1) In a 4- or 5-quart Dutch oven, cook the bacon over medium heat until
brown and crisp, 4 to 5 minutes. Using a slotted spoon, transfer the bacon to
paper towels to drain.

2) Add the onions to the pot and sprinkle with the sugar. Cook, stirring
often, until nicely brown, 3 to 5 minutes. Remove the onions with a slotted
spoon and set aside.

3) Melt 1 tablespoon of the butter in the pot over medium heat and add
the mushrooms. Cook, stirring often, until they give up their juices and the liquid
evaporates, 5 to 7 minutes. Remove the mushrooms with a slotted spoon and
set aside.

4) Rinse the chicken under cold running water and pat dry. Mix ¼ cup of the flour, the salt, and pepper in a paper bag. Add the chicken to the bag, a few pieces at a time, and shake until well coated. Shake off any excess flour mixture.

5) Heat the oil in the pot over medium-high heat. Add the chicken, in batches if necessary, and cook, turning, until nicely browned, about 10 minutes per batch. Remove the chicken and set aside. Drain off all but 1 teaspoon of the fat from the pot.

6) Add the mustard and tomato paste to the pot and cook, stirring, over medium-high heat 1 minute. Whisk in the beef broth and wine and bring to a boil, scraping up any brown bits from the bottom of the pot.

7) Return the bacon, onions, mushrooms, and chicken to the pot and bring to a boil. Reduce the heat to medium-low. Cover and simmer until the chicken is white throughout but still juicy, 20 to 30 minutes.

8) Transfer the chicken to a warm serving platter. Using your fingers or a spoon, knead the remaining 2 teaspoons flour into the remaining 1 teaspoon butter. Stir into the sauce with the thyme and bring to a boil over medium-high heat. Cook, stirring, until the sauce has thickened, 3 to 5 minutes. Sprinkle with the parsley just before serving.

Ground Chicken and Macaroni Scramble

T*his sort of supper has been a staple of busy home cooks for a couple of generations. In this nineties' version, I've used low-fat ground chicken instead of beef and eliminated the step of precooking the pasta.*

Makes 4 servings

1 tablespoon olive oil
1 pound ground chicken
1 onion, chopped
½ teaspoon salt
¼ teaspoon pepper
1 (26-ounce) jar spaghetti sauce
¾ cup dry red or white wine

1½ cups elbow macaroni
1 (11-ounce) can corn kernels, drained
1 (2¼-ounce) can sliced pitted ripe olives, drained
2 cups shredded Cheddar cheese (about 8 ounces)

1) In a 4- or 5-quart Dutch oven, heat the olive oil over medium heat. Add the chicken, onion, salt, and pepper and cook, stirring to break up the meat, until the chicken has lost all trace of pink and the onion is softened, about 7 minutes.

2) Whisk in the spaghetti sauce, wine, and ¾ cup water until well blended. Stir in the macaroni and bring to a boil. Reduce the heat to low, stir in the corn and olives, and cook until the macaroni is tender, 30 to 35 minutes.

3) Stir in 1 cup of the cheese and sprinkle the remaining 1 cup cheese over the top. Cover and cook until the cheese is melted, about 2 minutes.

Braised Chicken with Onions, Potatoes, and Peas

*T*he long, slow cooking of this old-fashioned supper is not only easy on the cook, it fills your kitchen with warm and comforting aromas.   ***Makes 4 servings***

1 (3½-pound) chicken, cut into
  8 pieces
2 tablespoons sweet Hungarian
  paprika
1½ teaspoons salt
1 teaspoon pepper
6 large onions (about 3 pounds),
  thinly sliced

1 cup chicken broth
12 small red potatoes (about
  1 pound), unpeeled and cut in
  half
1 (10-ounce) package frozen peas,
  thawed
2 tablespoons chopped parsley

1) Rinse the chicken under cold running water and pat dry. Season with the paprika, salt, and pepper.

2) Place half of the onions in the bottom of a 5-quart Dutch oven. Arrange the chicken pieces over the onions in a single layer. Top with the remaining onions. Pour in the chicken broth, cover, and cook over medium-low heat 1½ hours.

3) Arrange the potatoes on top of the chicken and cook, uncovered, until the potatoes are tender and the chicken is white throughout but still juicy, about 30 minutes longer. Scatter the peas over the top, cover, and cook, stirring occasionally, until heated through, about 2 minutes. Serve in soup plates and garnish with the parsley.

Chicken Paprikash

Serve this creamy stew over wide egg noodles to sop up the delicious sauce. **Makes 4 servings**

1 (3½-pound) chicken, cut into
  8 pieces
1 teaspoon salt
¼ teaspoon pepper
2 tablespoons vegetable oil
2 medium onions, sliced about
  ¼ inch thick
1 medium red bell pepper, cut
  into strips about 2 inches long
  and ¼ inch wide
2 tablespoons plus 1 teaspoon
  sweet Hungarian paprika

⅛ teaspoon cayenne
1 (14½-ounce) can diced
  tomatoes, drained
½ cup chicken broth
1½ teaspoons flour
½ cup sour cream, or more to
  taste
1½ teaspoons chopped fresh
  thyme or ½ teaspoon dried

1) Rinse the chicken under cold running water and pat dry. Season with the salt and pepper. In a 4- or 5-quart Dutch oven, heat the oil over medium heat. Add the chicken, in batches if necessary, and cook, turning, until nicely browned, about 10 minutes. Remove the chicken and set aside. Drain off and discard all but 2 tablespoons of the fat from the pot.

2) Add the onions and bell pepper to the pot and cook, stirring occasionally, over medium heat until softened, about 5 minutes. Stir in the paprika and cayenne and cook 2 minutes longer. Add the tomatoes and chicken broth. Increase the heat to high and bring to a boil, scraping up any brown bits from the bottom of the pot. Return the chicken to the pot and bring to a boil. Reduce the heat to medium-low, cover, and simmer until the chicken is white throughout but still juicy, 20 to 30 minutes.

3) Transfer the chicken to a warm serving platter. Mix the flour into the sour cream until well blended. Stir the sour cream mixture and thyme into the sauce and cook until just heated through, about 2 minutes. (Do not let the mixture boil.) Pour the sauce over the chicken and serve at once.

Chicken with Italian Sausage and Big Noodles

T*here's no need to precook the pasta for this satisfying meal—everything simmers together in the pot.*

Makes 4 servings

1 tablespoon olive oil
2 sweet Italian sausages (about
  6 ounces), removed from the
  casings and crumbled
1 large onion, chopped
2 large garlic cloves, minced
4 chicken thighs (about 1 pound)
4 chicken drumsticks (about
  1 pound)
1 teaspoon salt
½ teaspoon pepper

1 (28-ounce) can diced tomatoes,
  juices reserved
1 (15-ounce) can tomato sauce
½ cup dry red or white wine
6 ounces extra-wide egg noodles
  (about 4 cups)
1 tablespoon chopped fresh basil
  or 1 teaspoon dried
⅛ teaspoon crushed hot red
  pepper
¼ cup grated Parmesan cheese

1) In a 4- or 5-quart Dutch oven, heat the olive oil over medium heat. Add the sausage, onion, and garlic, stirring often, until the sausage is browned and cooked through, 5 to 7 minutes. Remove the sausage with a slotted spoon and set aside.

2) Rinse the chicken under cold running water and pat dry. Season with the salt and pepper. Add the chicken to the pot, in batches if necessary, and cook, turning, until nicely browned, about 10 minutes. Remove the chicken and set aside. Drain off and discard the fat in the pot.

3) Add the diced tomatoes with their juices, the tomato sauce, and wine to the pot. Bring to a boil over medium-high heat, scraping up any brown bits from the bottom of the pot. Stir in the noodles, basil, and crushed red pepper. Return the chicken to the pot and bring to a boil. Reduce the heat to medium-low, cover, and cook until the noodles are tender and the chicken is white throughout but still juicy, 20 to 30 minutes. Sprinkle with the Parmesan cheese just before serving.

Hawaiian Chicken and Rice

The mere allusion to anything
*Hawaiian conjures up pleasant images of leisurely sun-kissed
afternoons and balmy tropical breezes. This is not a bad reverie
after a particularly frenzied day. So go ahead and pull out the Don
Ho records while you wait for this comforting meal—you deserve it.*

Makes 4 servings

4 chicken breast halves on the
  bone (about 2 pounds)
¾ teaspoon salt
1½ tablespoons vegetable oil
2 tablespoons butter
1 medium onion, chopped (about
  1 cup)
1 medium red or green bell
  pepper, cut into ½-inch squares
  (about 1 cup)
1 cup long-grain white rice

1¾ cups chicken broth
⅓ cup pineapple juice
1 tablespoon soy sauce
¼ teaspoon ground ginger
Dash of cayenne
1 (8-ounce) can unsweetened
  pineapple tidbits, drained
2 tablespoons chopped cilantro or
  parsley
3 tablespoons coarsely chopped
  macadamia nuts

1) Rinse the chicken under cold running water and pat dry. Season with
the salt.

2) In a 4- or 5-quart Dutch oven, heat the oil over medium heat. Add the
chicken and cook, turning, until nicely browned on both sides, 8 to 10 minutes.
Remove the chicken and set aside. Drain and discard the fat from the pot.

3) Melt the butter in the same pan over medium heat. Add the onion and
bell pepper and cook, stirring occasionally, until softened but not browned,
3 to 5 minutes. Stir in the rice to coat well. Stir in the chicken broth, pineapple
juice, soy sauce, ginger, and cayenne and bring to a boil over medium-high
heat, scraping up any browned bits from the bottom of the pot. Return the
chicken to the pot, skin side down, and bring the liquid to a boil. Reduce the
heat to medium-low, cover, and cook until the chicken is white throughout
but still juicy, 20 to 30 minutes.

4) Transfer the chicken to a warm platter. Reduce the heat to low. Add the pineapple and cilantro to the rice mixture remaining in the pan and cook, uncovered, until most of the liquid has been absorbed and the pineapple is heated through, 1 to 2 minutes. Sprinkle the macadamia nuts on top just before serving.

Polenta and Chicken Torta

his is delicious straight from the pot while the polenta is still soft, but for the sake of convenience I've added an extra step so it can be prepared in advance and served in a more elegant fashion.

Makes 4 to 6 servings

2 skinless, boneless chicken
  breast halves (about ¾ pound)
¾ teaspoon salt
¼ teaspoon pepper
1 tablespoon olive oil
1 large garlic clove, minced
3 cups chicken broth
1 cup milk
1 cup instant polenta or yellow
  cornmeal

½ cup grated Parmesan cheese
4 tablespoons butter, cut into bits
10 kalamata olives (about ¼ cup),
  pitted and coarsely chopped
3 tablespoons oil-packed sun-
  dried tomatoes, drained
1½ tablespoons chopped fresh
  basil or parsley

1) Rinse the chicken under cold running water and pat dry. Cut into bite-size pieces. Season with ¼ teaspoon of the salt and the pepper. In a large saucepan or Dutch oven, heat the olive oil over medium-high heat. Add the garlic and cook until just fragrant, about 30 seconds. Add the chicken and cook, stirring, until lightly browned outside and white throughout but still juicy, 3 to 4 minutes. Remove the chicken and set aside. Drain off any oil left in the pan.

2) If you plan on letting the polenta cool to serve later, use a 22-inch piece of heavy-duty plastic wrap to line the inside of a 9-inch round cake pan, letting the excess plastic drape over the edges. Set aside.

3) In the same saucepan, combine the chicken broth, milk, and the remaining ½ teaspoon salt. Bring to a boil over medium-high heat. Whisk in the polenta in a slow steady stream. Reduce the heat to medium and cook, stirring constantly, until the polenta is thickened to the consistency of hot cereal, about 5 minutes. Remove the pan from the heat and stir in the chicken, cheese, butter, olives, sun-dried tomatoes, and basil. Serve at once or proceed to the next step.

4) Pour the polenta mixture into the prepared pan, taking care not to disturb the plastic wrap. Using your fingers or the back of a spoon, pat the mixture into an even layer. Cover with excess plastic wrap and let cool. Refrigerate until firm, about 1 hour, or as long as 2 days.

5) Preheat the oven to 400 degrees F. Unmold the polenta onto a foil- or parchment-lined baking sheet. Discard the plastic wrap. Bake about 30 minutes, or until heated through and golden around the edges. Cut into wedges and serve warm.

Chicken à la Brunswick

T*his is a streamlined version of a stew that originated in Brunswick County, Virginia, more than 100 years ago. The original recipe called for squirrel, but as wild game became scarce, chicken was substituted. Serve this with corn bread and honey for a Southern-style feast.* ***Makes 4 servings***

1 (3½-pound) chicken, cut into 8 pieces
¾ teaspoon salt
3 bacon slices, cut into ½-inch pieces
1 large onion, cut into slices ½ inch thick
1 (14½-ounce) can diced tomatoes, drained
2 medium red potatoes (about ¾ pound), peeled and cut into ½-inch cubes

1 (10-ounce) package frozen corn kernels
1 (10-ounce) package frozen lima beans
½ cup chicken broth
⅛ teaspoon cayenne
⅛ teaspoon sugar

1) Rinse the chicken under cold running water and pat dry. Season with the salt. Set aside.

2) In a 4- or 5-quart Dutch oven, cook the bacon over medium heat until browned and crisp, 4 to 5 minutes. Using a slotted spoon, transfer the bacon to paper towels to drain.

3) Add the chicken to the hot bacon drippings, in batches if necessary, and cook over medium heat, turning, until nicely browned, about 10 minutes. Remove the chicken and set aside. Drain off all but 2 tablespoons of the fat from the pot.

4) Add the onion to the pot and cook, stirring occasionally, until softened but not browned, 3 to 5 minutes. Stir in the tomatoes, potatoes, frozen corn, frozen lima beans, chicken broth, cayenne, and sugar. Bring to a boil over medium-high heat, breaking apart the blocks of frozen vegetables and scraping up any brown bits from the bottom of the pan. Return the chicken to the pot and bring to a boil. Reduce the heat to medium-low, cover, and cook until the potatoes are tender and the chicken is white throughout but still juicy, 20 to 30 minutes.

5) Using a slotted spoon, remove the chicken and most of the vegetables to a warm serving platter. Bring the liquid and the remaining vegetables to a boil over high heat. Cook, stirring occasionally, until the sauce is thick enough to coat the back of a spoon, 8 to 10 minutes. Spoon the sauce over the chicken and vegetables and top with the reserved bacon pieces.

Spring Chicken Risotto

*C*ome spring, I think a bowl of
creamy risotto dotted with juicy chunks of chicken and tender
asparagus spears is about as good as things can get. Arborio rice can
be found in Italian delicatessens as well as many supermarkets.

Makes 4 servings

3 skinless, boneless chicken
   breast halves (about 1 pound)
½ teaspoon salt
¼ teaspoon pepper
1½ tablespoons olive oil
2 garlic cloves, minced
1 pound fresh asparagus or
   1 (10-ounce) package frozen
   asparagus tips, thawed

2 tablespoons unsalted butter
1 small onion, finely chopped
1 cup Arborio rice
½ cup dry white wine
4 cups hot chicken broth
½ cup grated Parmesan or aged
   Asiago cheese
1 tablespoon chopped chives

1) Rinse the chicken under cold running water and pat dry. Cut into
¾-inch pieces and season with the salt and pepper.

2) In a 4-quart Dutch oven or heavy-bottomed nonreactive saucepan, heat
1 tablespoon of the olive oil over medium-high heat. Stir in the garlic and cook
until fragrant, about 30 seconds. Add the chicken and cook, stirring
occasionally, until lightly browned outside and white throughout but still juicy,
3 to 4 minutes. Remove the chicken and set aside.

3) If using fresh asparagus, trim off and discard the tough ends. Cut the
asparagus diagonally into 1-inch pieces, leaving the tips intact. Add the
remaining ½ tablespoon olive oil to the pot and heat over medium heat. Add
the asparagus and cook, stirring often, until crisp-tender, 2 to 3 minutes.
Remove the asparagus and set aside.

4) In the same pot, melt the butter over medium heat. Add the onion and
cook, stirring occasionally, until softened but not browned, 3 to 5 minutes. Add
the rice and cook, stirring often, until translucent and coated with the butter,
about 2 minutes.

5) Pour in the wine and bring to a boil over high heat, scraping up any brown bits from the bottom of the pan. Cook, stirring often, until the wine is absorbed, 1 to 2 minutes. Reduce the heat to medium. Pour in 1 cup of the hot chicken broth and cook, stirring often, until absorbed. Continue adding broth, 1 cup at a time, stirring often, until the broth is absorbed and the rice is creamy and tender but still firm in the center, about 15 minutes total.

6) Stir in the chicken and asparagus and cook until heated through, 1 to 2 minutes. Stir in the Parmesan cheese and top with chopped chives just before serving. Serve at once.

Chicken Thighs with Swiss Chard and Sausage

Serve this Italian stew in soup plates with some good crusty bread on the side.

Makes 4 to 6 servings

1 (1-pound) bunch of Swiss chard, leaves and stems cut crosswise
6 chicken thighs on the bone (about 1½ pounds)
1 teaspoon salt
½ teaspoon pepper
2½ tablespoons olive oil
6 sweet Italian sausages (about 1 pound)
1 large onion, chopped
2 garlic cloves, minced

12 small red potatoes (about 1 pound), unpeeled and cut in half
6 medium carrots (about 1 pound), peeled and cut into 1½-inch pieces
2 cups chicken broth
1 (14½-ounce) can diced tomatoes, drained
⅛ teaspoon crushed hot red pepper
Dash of grated nutmeg

1) In a 5-quart Dutch oven three-quarters full of boiling salted water, cook the Swiss chard over high heat until just barely tender, about 5 minutes. Drain, rinse under cold running water to cool, and squeeze out the excess liquid.

2) Rinse the chicken under cold running water and pat dry. Season with the salt and pepper. In the same pot, heat 1½ tablespoons of the olive oil over medium-high heat. Add the chicken and cook, turning, until nicely browned, about 10 minutes. Remove the chicken and set aside.

3) Prick the sausages with a fork. In the same pot, cook the sausages over medium heat, turning, until lightly browned, about 5 minutes. Remove the sausages and set aside. Drain off and discard any fat from the pot.

4) Heat the remaining 1 tablespoon olive oil over medium heat. Add the onion and garlic and cook, stirring occasionally, until softened, 3 to 5 minutes. Add the chard, chicken, sausages, potatoes, carrots, chicken broth, tomatoes, crushed red pepper, and nutmeg. Bring to a boil. Reduce the heat to low, cover, and cook 45 minutes.

Mexicali Chicken Stew

Boneless chicken breasts speed up the cooking time, so this hearty stew can be ready in less than an hour.

Makes 4 servings

1 tablespoon vegetable oil
1 medium onion, finely chopped
1 jalapeño or serrano pepper,
  seeded and minced
2 garlic cloves, minced
8 tomatillos (about ½ pound),
  husked, rinsed, and finely
  chopped, or 1 (12-ounce) can,
  drained and finely chopped
4 celery ribs, finely chopped
2 medium carrots, peeled and
  finely chopped
1 (4-ounce) can diced green chiles
1½ teaspoons ground cumin

Dash of cayenne
5 cups chicken broth and/or
  water
4 skinless, boneless chicken
  breast halves (about
  1½ pounds)
1 teaspoon salt
¼ teaspoon pepper
½ cup coarsely chopped cilantro
  plus 4 sprigs for garnish
Hot cooked long-grain white rice
½ cup sour cream
¼ cup salsa
Lime wedges

1) In a large Dutch oven, heat the oil over medium heat. Add the onion, jalapeño pepper, and garlic and cook, stirring occasionally, until softened but not browned, 3 to 5 minutes. Add the tomatillos, celery, and carrots and cook, stirring occasionally, until the vegetables are crisp-tender, about 3 minutes. Stir in the chiles with their juices, the cumin, cayenne, and 4 cups of the chicken broth. Bring to a boil over medium-high heat. Reduce the heat to medium-low and cook, stirring occasionally, until thickened, 15 to 20 minutes.

2) Cut the chicken into ¾-inch pieces. Season with the salt and pepper. Add the chicken and the remaining 1 cup broth to the pot and bring to a boil over medium-high heat. Reduce the heat to low and simmer 20 minutes. Stir in the chopped cilantro and cook 1 minute longer.

3) Serve over the rice. Top each serving with 2 tablespoons sour cream and 1 tablespoon salsa. Garnish with the cilantro sprigs and lime wedges.

Chicken with Tomatoes, Olives, and White Wine

Makes 4 servings

1 (3½-pound) chicken, cut into
  8 pieces
2 tablespoons lemon juice
2 teaspoons dried thyme
1 teaspoon salt
½ teaspoon pepper
2 tablespoons olive oil
¼ pound lean salt pork, cut into
  ½-inch dice
2 large onions, chopped
3 garlic cloves, thinly sliced

2 pounds tomatoes, peeled,
  seeded, and quartered, or
  1 (28-ounce) can peeled plum
  tomatoes, drained and coarsely
  chopped
½ cup dry white wine
2 bay leaves
⅓ cup Niçoise olives (about
  2 ounces), pitted, or ½ cup
  oil-cured olives, pitted
⅓ cup chopped parsley

1) Rinse the chicken and pat dry. In a large bowl, combine the chicken with the lemon juice and thyme. Cover and marinate 2 hours at room temperature.

2) Pat the chicken dry and season with the salt and pepper. In a 5-quart Dutch oven, heat the olive oil over medium-high heat. Add the chicken, in batches if necessary, and the salt pork and cook, turning, until nicely browned, about 10 minutes. Using a slotted spoon, remove the chicken and salt pork and set aside. Pour off and discard all but 1½ tablespoons of the fat from the pot.

3) Add the onions and garlic to the pot and cook over medium heat, stirring occasionally, until softened but not browned, 3 to 5 minutes. Stir in the tomatoes, wine, and bay leaves and cook until the mixture is reduced and slightly thickened, about 10 minutes. Return the chicken and salt pork to the pot. Reduce the heat to low and cook, uncovered, basting frequently, until the chicken is white throughout but still juicy, 25 to 35 minutes.

4) Stir in the olives and cook until heated through, about 5 minutes longer. Remove the chicken to a warm serving platter and discard the bay leaves. Pour the sauce over the chicken, garnish with the parsley, and serve.

Country Captain

Hot cooked rice and mango chutney are natural accompaniments to this classic chicken stew with its Indian overtones.

Makes 4 servings

⅓ cup slivered almonds
1 (3½-pound) chicken, cut into
  8 pieces
¼ cup flour
1 teaspoon salt
½ teaspoon pepper
2 tablespoons vegetable oil
1 large onion, chopped

1 small green bell pepper, cut into
  ½-inch squares
2 garlic cloves, minced
1 tablespoon curry powder
1 (14½-ounce) can stewed
  tomatoes
½ cup golden or dark raisins
½ teaspoon dried thyme leaves

1) In a dry 5-quart Dutch oven, toast the almonds over medium heat, stirring constantly, until lightly browned, 3 to 4 minutes. Remove the almonds from the pan and set aside to cool.

2) Rinse the chicken under cold running water and pat dry. Mix the flour, salt, and pepper in a paper bag. Add the chicken pieces, a few at a time, to the bag and shake to coat evenly. Shake off any excess flour mixture.

3) In the same Dutch oven, heat the oil over medium-high heat. Add the chicken, in batches if necessary, and cook, turning, until nicely browned, about 10 minutes per batch. Remove the chicken and set aside. Drain off and discard all but 1 tablespoon of the fat from the pot.

4) Add the onion, bell pepper, garlic, and curry powder. Reduce the heat to medium and cook, stirring occasionally, until the vegetables are softened but not browned, 3 to 5 minutes. Stir in the tomatoes and bring to a boil, scraping up any brown bits from the bottom of the pot. Return the chicken to the pot and reduce the heat to low. Cook, partially covered, until the chicken is white throughout but still juicy, 20 to 30 minutes.

5) Transfer the chicken to a warm serving platter. Increase the heat to high and add the raisins and the thyme. Cook, stirring often, until the sauce has thickened slightly, about 2 minutes. Pour the sauce over the chicken and sprinkle with the toasted almonds.

Chicken Fricassee with Vegetables

Fricassees, which are poultry stews bound with cream sauce, had their heyday in the middle of this century. Although such fare is not presently at its height of popularity, one bite will remind you why this sort of comfort food will never go away.

Makes 4 servings

1 (3½-pound) chicken, cut into 8 pieces
1 teaspoon salt
½ teaspoon pepper
2 tablespoons vegetable oil
4 tablespoons unsalted butter
¼ pound button mushrooms, cut in half
3 carrots, peeled and cut diagonally into slices about ¼ inch thick

1 medium onion, finely chopped
1 celery rib, finely chopped
3 tablespoons flour
2½ cups chicken broth
½ cup dry white wine
½ cup heavy cream
1 (10-ounce) package frozen peas and pearl onions, thawed
1 tablespoon chopped fresh thyme or 1 teaspoon dried
2 tablespoons chopped parsley

1) Rinse the chicken under cold running water and pat dry. Season with the salt and pepper. In a 4- or 5-quart Dutch oven, heat the oil over medium heat. Add the chicken, in batches if necessary, and cook, turning, until nicely browned, about 10 minutes. Remove the chicken and set aside. Drain off all the cooking fat from the pot.

2) In the same pot, melt 1 tablespoon of the butter over medium heat. Add the mushrooms and cook, stirring occasionally, until they give up their juices and the liquid evaporates, 5 to 7 minutes. Remove the mushrooms with a slotted spoon and set aside.

3) Melt the remaining 3 tablespoons butter in the pot over medium heat. Add the carrots, onion, and celery and cook, stirring occasionally, until softened but not browned, about 5 minutes. Add the flour and cook, stirring constantly, 1 minute longer. Whisk in the chicken broth and wine and bring to a boil, scraping up any brown bits from the bottom of the pot. Return the chicken to the pot and bring to a simmer. Reduce the heat to medium-low, partially cover, and cook until the chicken is white throughout but still juicy, 20 to 30 minutes. Remove the chicken to a warm deep bowl or platter.

4) Increase the heat to high and bring the cooking liquid to a boil. Cook until thickened and reduced by one-third, about 8 minutes. Reduce the heat to medium. Add the cream and simmer until the sauce thickens slightly, about 3 minutes. Stir in the mushrooms, peas and pearl onions, and thyme and cook until just heated through, 3 to 5 minutes. Pour the sauce over the chicken and top with the chopped parsley.

Chicken Cacciatore

*I*n *this recipe, another Italian standby, zucchini, is added to a classically inspired dish. A crusty loaf of garlic bread and a tossed green salad are all that is needed for a hearty feast.* **Makes 4 servings**

1 (3½-pound) chicken, cut into
   8 pieces
1 teaspoon salt
¼ teaspoon pepper
2 tablespoons olive oil
1 large onion, chopped
3 medium zucchini (about
   1 pound), cut into slices about
   ¼ inch thick
½ pound mushrooms, preferably
   Italian brown (cremini), cut into
   halves or quarters

3 garlic cloves, minced
1 (14½-ounce) can diced
   tomatoes, drained
1 cup dry red wine
1 tablespoon chopped fresh basil
   or 1 teaspoon dried
2 tablespoons chopped parsley

1) Rinse the chicken under cold running water and pat dry. Season with the salt and pepper. In a 4- or 5-quart Dutch oven, heat the olive oil over medium heat. Add the chicken, in batches if necessary, and cook, turning, until nicely browned, about 10 minutes. Remove the chicken and set aside.

2) Add the onion to the pot and cook, stirring occasionally, until just softened, about 2 minutes. Add the zucchini, mushrooms, and garlic and cook, stirring occasionally, 5 minutes longer.

3) Stir in the tomatoes, wine, and basil. Increase the heat to medium-high and bring to a boil, scraping up any brown bits from the bottom of the pot. Return the chicken to the pot and bring to a boil. Reduce the heat to medium-low, cover, and simmer until the chicken is white throughout but still juicy, 20 to 30 minutes. Garnish with the parsley just before serving.

Simply Wonderful Cassoulet

This simple adaptation of the *long-simmering French classic stew is a hearty and satisfying supper for a cool winter day.*
Makes 6 servings

1 (1-pound) package dried white beans, such as Great Northern
5 cups chicken broth and/or water
7 or 8 skinless, boneless chicken thighs (about 1½ pounds)
6 medium carrots (about 1 pound), peeled and coarsely chopped
½ pound Polish kielbasa sausage, cut diagonally into ¼-inch-thick slices
¼ pound cooked ham, cut into ½-inch dice

4 medium celery ribs, coarsely chopped
1 large onion, coarsely chopped
1 (14½-ounce) can diced tomatoes, drained
1½ cups dry white wine
1 tablespoon chopped fresh thyme or 1 teaspoon dried
5 garlic cloves, minced
2 bay leaves
1½ teaspoons salt
½ teaspoon pepper
¾ cup plain dried bread crumbs
3 tablespoons chopped parsley

1) Rinse the beans in a colander under cold running water. Pick them over and discard any grit. Place the beans in a 5-quart ovenproof Dutch oven or flameproof casserole and add enough cold water to cover by at least 2 inches. Let the beans soak overnight. (Alternatively, bring them to a boil over high heat. Cover, remove from the heat, and let stand 1 hour.)

2) Preheat the oven to 350 degrees F. Drain and rinse the beans. Return them to the pot, pour in the chicken broth, and bring to a boil over high heat.

3) Rinse the chicken under cold running water and pat dry. Cut into 2-inch pieces and stir into the beans. Add the carrots, sausage, ham, celery, onion, tomatoes, wine, thyme, garlic, bay leaves, salt, and pepper. Return to a boil.

4) Cover and bake 1½ hours. Remove and discard the bay leaves. Sprinkle on the bread crumbs. Bake, uncovered, until the top is lightly browned and the beans are tender, 20 to 30 minutes. Sprinkle the parsley on top before serving.

Chicken Soup with Rice and Escarole

Look for heads of escarole near *the lettuce in your produce market. If it is not available, substitute spinach, Swiss chard, or kale.*   ***Makes 4 to 6 servings***

6 cups chicken broth
1 cup Arborio or long-grain white
   rice
3 garlic cloves, thinly sliced
3 skinless, boneless chicken
   breast halves (about 1 pound),
   cut into ½-inch dice

2 cups (packed) coarsely chopped
   fresh escarole
Salt and coarsely ground pepper
Grated Parmesan cheese

1) In a 5- or 6-quart soup pot, bring the chicken broth and 2 cups water to a boil over high heat. Add the rice and garlic and reduce heat to medium. Cook, uncovered, until the rice is barely tender, about 10 minutes.

2) Add the chicken and escarole and reduce heat to medium-low. Cook until the chicken is white throughout but still juicy and the escarole is tender, about 7 minutes. Season with salt and pepper to taste. Pass a bowl of grated Parmesan cheese at the table.

Chicken in a Pasta Pot

America's love affair with pasta may have begun when Lady and the Tramp shared a plate of spaghetti and meatballs on the silver screen. Or maybe it started when starving students finally found an affordable dining option. Nevertheless, ever since travel abroad became more affordable, there's been no stopping our curiosity about this simple and satisfying way to eat a meal. We now recognize that in addition to being healthy, filling, and economical, pasta can be anything from a quick and carefree dinner to something downright elegant.

Pasta should be cooked in the biggest pot you've got—give the pasta plenty of room to "roll with the moves" of the water, so it rids itself of starch and doesn't clump together. Make sure the water is at a full boil over high heat before adding the pasta.

Except for tortellini, which I purchase either fresh or frozen, all the recipes in this chapter were tested with a good brand of dried pasta from the supermarket. A quality fresh pasta is fine to use, though often less readily available—just remember that it is perishable and that it cooks in 1 to 3 minutes.

A trip through the next few pages will show you that just because it's pasta doesn't mean it has to be Italian. Take a ride through the southwest with Spaghetti Western and breeze through California with Chicken in a Field of Green Linguine. Raid the summer garden for Fusilli with Chicken, Zucchini, and Tomatoes and savor the pleasantly strong and grown-up flavors of Orecchiette with Chicken, Broccoli Rabe, and Gorgonzola.

My favorite thing about these recipes is that all you need in order to get started is one big pot and a colander. So put on the water to boil—dinner is only a few minutes away. And while you're at it, make mine Fettuccine with Chicken in Sun-Dried Tomato Cream.

Bow Ties With Creamy Chicken and Mushrooms

When wild mushrooms are available, by all means include a few in this sauce. Their woodsy flavor is incomparable.

Makes 4 servings

1 pound bow-tie pasta (farfalle)
3 skinless, boneless chicken
   breast halves (about 1 pound)
1 teaspoon salt
½ teaspoon pepper
2 tablespoons olive oil
2 tablespoons unsalted butter

3 medium shallots, minced
¾ pound sliced mushrooms
½ cup chicken broth
¼ cup heavy cream
1½ teaspoons chopped fresh
   thyme or ½ teaspoon dried
Grated Parmesan cheese

1) In a large pot of boiling salted water, cook the pasta until tender but still firm, about 10 minutes. Rinse and drain well.

2) Rinse the chicken under cold running water and pat dry. Cut into thin strips and season with ½ teaspoon of the salt and ¼ teaspoon of the pepper.

3) In the same pot, heat the olive oil over medium heat. Cook the chicken, stirring, until white throughout but still juicy, 3 to 5 minutes. Remove the chicken and set aside.

4) Melt the butter in the same pot over medium heat. Add the shallots and cook until softened, about 1 minute. Add the mushrooms and cook, stirring often, until they give up their juices and the liquid evaporates, 5 to 7 minutes.

5) Stir in the chicken broth and cream and bring to a boil over medium-high heat. Reduce the heat to low and stir in the pasta, chicken, the remaining ½ teaspoon salt and ¼ teaspoon pepper, and the thyme. Cook, tossing lightly, until heated through, 1 to 2 minutes. Serve at once. Pass a bowl of grated Parmesan cheese at the table.

Pasta with Spring Chicken and Vegetables

Makes 4 servings

1 pound bow-tie pasta (farfalle)
3 skinless, boneless chicken
  breast halves (about 1 pound)
1 teaspoon salt
¼ teaspoon pepper
3 tablespoons unsalted butter
1 tablespoon olive oil
2 medium shallots, finely chopped
2 medium carrots, peeled and
  thinly sliced

1 pound fresh asparagus, cut
  diagonally into 1-inch lengths,
  or 1 (10-ounce) package frozen
  asparagus tips, thawed
2 cups chicken broth
1 (10-ounce) package frozen peas,
  thawed
¼ cup chopped fresh basil or
  parsley
Grated Parmesan cheese

1) In a large pot of boiling salted water, cook the pasta until tender but still firm, about 10 minutes. Rinse and drain well.

2) Rinse the chicken under cold running water and pat dry. Cut into ¾-inch pieces and season with ½ teaspoon of the salt and the pepper.

3) In the same pot, melt 1 tablespoon of the butter in the oil over medium heat. Add the chicken and cook, stirring, until white throughout but still juicy, 3 to 4 minutes. Remove the chicken and set aside.

4) Melt the remaining 2 tablespoons butter in the same pot over medium heat. Add the shallots and cook, stirring often, until softened but not browned, 1 to 2 minutes. Stir in the carrots and asparagus and cook, stirring often, 1 minute. Add the chicken broth, increase the heat to high, and cook until the vegetables are crisp-tender and the broth is reduced to 1¼ cups, about 3 minutes.

5) Stir in the peas and reduce the heat to low. Add the pasta, chicken, the remaining ½ teaspoon salt, and the basil. Cook, tossing lightly, until heated through, 1 to 2 minutes. Serve at once. Pass a bowl of grated Parmesan cheese at the table.

Bow Ties with Spicy Chicken, Pepper, and Tomatoes

Makes 4 servings

1 pound bow-tie pasta (farfalle)
3 skinless, boneless chicken
   breast halves (about 1 pound)
1 teaspoon salt
¼ cup olive oil
4 garlic cloves, thinly sliced
1 large red bell pepper, cut into
   ½-inch squares

1 (28-ounce) can diced tomatoes,
   drained
½ teaspoon crushed hot red
   pepper, or to taste
¼ cup chopped parsley
Grated Parmesan cheese

1) In a large pot of boiling salted water, cook the pasta until tender but still firm, about 10 minutes. Rinse and drain well.

2) Rinse the chicken under cold running water and pat dry. Cut into ³⁄₄-inch pieces and season with ½ teaspoon of the salt.

3) In the same pot, heat 2 tablespoons of the olive oil over medium heat. Add the chicken and cook, stirring, until white throughout but still juicy, 3 to 4 minutes. Remove the chicken and set aside.

4) Heat the remaining olive oil in the same pot over medium heat. Add the garlic and red bell pepper and cook, stirring occasionally, until softened but not browned, 3 to 5 minutes. Add the remaining ½ teaspoon salt, the tomatoes, and crushed red pepper and cook until slightly thickened, 5 to 7 minutes.

5) Reduce the heat to low. Add the pasta, chicken, and parsley and cook, tossing lightly, until heated through, 1 to 2 minutes. Serve at once. Pass a bowl of grated Parmesan cheese at the table.

Pasta with Chicken Puttanesca

Puttanesca sauce, like the *"working girls" for whom it is named, is hot, spicy, and fast. Nuggets of juicy chicken only make it better. Anchovy lovers can apply the olive oil from the anchovies toward the amount called for in the recipe.* **Makes 4 servings**

1 pound creste di gallo (pasta shaped like roosters' combs) or other hollow pasta with ridges, such as rigatoni
3 skinless, boneless chicken breast halves (about 1 pound)
¼ teaspoon salt
¼ teaspoon pepper
½ cup extra-virgin olive oil
1 (2-ounce) can flat anchovy fillets, drained and coarsely chopped

3 large garlic cloves, minced
1 (14½-ounce) can diced tomatoes, drained
¼ to ½ teaspoon crushed hot red pepper, to taste
1 cup kalamata olives, pitted and coarsely chopped
2 tablespoons drained capers
¼ cup chopped parsley

1) In a large pot of boiling salted water, cook the pasta until tender but still firm, 8 to 10 minutes. Rinse and drain well.

2) Rinse the chicken under cold running water and pat dry. Cut into ¾-inch pieces and season with the salt and pepper.

3) In the same pot, heat 2 tablespoons of the olive oil over medium heat. Add the chicken and cook, stirring, until white throughout but still juicy, 3 to 4 minutes. Remove the chicken and set aside.

4) Add the anchovies and garlic and cook until fragrant, about 30 seconds. Add the remaining 6 tablespoons olive oil, the tomatoes, and crushed red pepper and cook, stirring occasionally, until slightly thickened, 7 to 9 minutes.

5) Reduce the heat to low. Add the pasta, chicken, olives, capers, and parsley. Cook, tossing lightly, until heated through, 1 to 2 minutes. Serve at once.

Fettuccine with Chicken in Sun-Dried Tomato Cream

Tomato-flavored pasta delivers a *double dose of sophistication to this rich and creamy entrée—by all means use it when possible.*   ***Makes 4 servings***

1 pound tomato or egg fettuccine
3 skinless, boneless chicken
   breast halves (about 1 pound)
¾ teaspoon salt
½ teaspoon coarsely ground
   pepper
1 tablespoon unsalted butter
1 tablespoon olive oil
1 medium shallot, finely chopped

1 cup heavy cream
1 cup chicken broth
12 oil-packed sun-dried tomato
   halves, drained and cut into thin
   strips
2 tablespoons chopped fresh basil
   or 1½ teaspoons dried
Fresh basil sprigs

1) In a large pot of boiling salted water, cook the pasta until tender but still firm, about 10 minutes. Rinse and drain well.

2) Rinse the chicken under cold running water and pat dry. Cut into thin strips and season with ½ teaspoon of the salt and ¼ teaspoon of the pepper.

3) In the same pot, melt the butter in olive oil over medium heat. Add the chicken and cook, stirring, until white throughout but still juicy, 3 to 5 minutes. Remove the chicken and set aside.

4) Add the shallot and cook over medium heat, stirring occasionally, until softened but not browned, 1 to 2 minutes. Add the cream and increase the heat to high. Bring to a boil and cook, stirring occasionally, until thickened and reduced by one-third, 5 to 7 minutes. Reduce the heat to low. Whisk in the chicken broth and cook, stirring occasionally, until heated through, about 5 minutes.

5) Stir in the pasta, chicken, the remaining ¼ teaspoon salt and ¼ teaspoon pepper, the sun-dried tomatoes, and basil and cook, tossing lightly, until heated through, 1 to 2 minutes. Garnish with the fresh basil sprigs. Serve at once.

Fusilli with Chicken, Zucchini, and Tomatoes

When your summer garden is *loaded with zucchini, this is an economical and delicious way to celebrate the season.*

Makes 4 servings

1 pound fusilli or other corkscrew-shaped pasta

3 skinless, boneless chicken breast halves (about 1 pound)

1 teaspoon salt

½ teaspoon pepper

⅔ cup olive oil

3 to 4 garlic cloves, minced

6 medium zucchini (about 2 pounds), cut into ½-inch dice

1 (28-ounce) can diced tomatoes, drained

1 tablespoon chopped fresh oregano or 1 teaspoon dried

Grated Romano or Parmesan cheese

1) In a large pot of boiling salted water, cook the pasta until tender but still firm, about 10 minutes. Rinse and drain well.

2) Rinse the chicken under cold running water and pat dry. Cut into ¾-inch pieces and season with ½ teaspoon of the salt and ¼ teaspoon of the pepper.

3) In the same pot, heat 2 tablespoons of the olive oil over medium heat. Add the chicken and cook, stirring, until white throughout but still juicy, 3 to 4 minutes. Remove the chicken and set aside.

4) Add the remaining olive oil to the pot and heat over medium heat. Add the garlic and cook until fragrant, about 30 seconds. Add the zucchini, tomatoes, and the remaining ½ teaspoon salt and ¼ teaspoon pepper. Cook, stirring frequently, until the zucchini is crisp-tender, 3 to 5 minutes.

5) Reduce the heat to low. Add the pasta, chicken, and oregano and cook, tossing lightly, until heated through, 1 to 2 minutes. Serve at once. Pass a bowl of grated Romano cheese at the table.

Chicken in a Field of
Green Linguine

Even the most modest herb
garden can produce enough fragrant green for this memorable tangle
of flavors. What you lack in variety, make up with parsley.

Makes 4 servings

1 pound spinach or egg linguine
3 skinless, boneless chicken
   breast halves (about 1 pound)
1 teaspoon salt
½ teaspoon paprika
¼ to ½ teaspoon coarsely ground
   pepper, to taste
¼ to ⅓ cup extra-virgin olive oil,
   to taste

3 garlic cloves, minced
½ cup assorted finely chopped
   fresh herbs, such as basil,
   chives, marjoram, oregano,
   rosemary, tarragon, thyme, and
   parsley
Grated Parmesan or Romano
   cheese

1) In a large pot of boiling salted water, cook the pasta until tender but still firm, about 10 minutes. Rinse and drain well.

2) Rinse the chicken under cold running water and pat dry. Cut into thin strips and season with ½ teaspoon of the salt, the paprika, and ¼ teaspoon of the pepper.

3) In the same pot, heat 2 tablespoons of the olive oil over medium heat. Add the garlic and cook until fragrant, about 30 seconds. Add the chicken and cook, stirring, until white throughout but still juicy, 3 to 5 minutes.

4) Reduce the heat to low. Add the remaining 2 tablespoons olive oil, the pasta, and the remaining ½ teaspoon salt and cook, tossing, until heated through, 1 to 2 minutes. Add the herbs and toss again. Taste, adding additional olive oil and pepper if needed. Serve at once. Pass a bowl of grated Parmesan cheese at the table.

Mostaccioli Mexicali

*A*fter a busy day, spice up your
life with this quick and easy entrée. The robust flavors belie its
simple preparation. **Makes 4 servings**

1 pound mostaccioli or other
    tube-shaped pasta
3 skinless, boneless chicken
    breast halves (about 1 pound)
¾ teaspoon salt
¼ teaspoon ground cumin
¼ teaspoon pepper

2 tablespoons olive oil
2 garlic cloves, minced
1 (24-ounce) jar thick 'n chunky-
    style salsa
1 cup crumbled feta cheese (about
    4 ounces)
¼ cup coarsely chopped cilantro

1) In a large pot of boiling salted water, cook the pasta until tender but still firm, about 10 minutes. Remove and drain well.

2) Rinse the chicken under cold running water and pat dry. Cut into ¾-inch pieces and season with the salt, cumin, and pepper.

3) In the same pot, heat the olive oil over medium heat. Add the garlic and cook until fragrant, about 30 seconds. Add the chicken and cook, stirring, until just white throughout, about 3 minutes. Add the salsa and cook, stirring occasionally, until heated through, 2 to 3 minutes.

4) Reduce the heat to low. Add the pasta and cheese and cook, tossing, until the pasta is heated through, 1 to 2 minutes. Sprinkle with the cilantro and serve at once.

Orecchiette with Chicken, Broccoli Rabe, and Gorgonzola

*T*hese chewy "little ears" of cup-shaped pasta are sometimes difficult to find. If that's the case, substitute penne or ziti in this full-flavored dish. ***Makes 4 servings***

2 bunches of broccoli rabe (1½ to 2 pounds)
1 pound orecchiette
3 skinless, boneless chicken breast halves (about 1 pound)
½ teaspoon salt
¼ teaspoon pepper

2 tablespoons olive oil
2 garlic cloves, minced
2 tablespoons unsalted butter
⅛ teaspoon crushed hot red pepper
1 cup crumbled Gorgonzola cheese (about 6 ounces)

1) In a large pot of boiling salted water, cook the broccoli rabe until tender, 8 to 10 minutes. Remove with a slotted spoon and drain in a colander. Chop coarsely and set aside.

2) Return the water to a full boil over high heat. Add the pasta and cook until tender but still firm, about 10 minutes. Rinse and drain well.

3) Rinse the chicken under cold running water and pat dry. Cut into ¾-inch pieces and season with the salt and pepper.

4) In the same pot, heat the olive oil over medium heat. Add the garlic and cook until fragrant, about 30 seconds. Add the chicken and cook, stirring, until white throughout, about 3 minutes. Add the butter and melt over medium heat. Add the broccoli rabe and crushed red pepper and cook, stirring occasionally, until well coated, 1 to 2 minutes.

5) Reduce the heat to low. Add the pasta and Gorgonzola cheese and cook, tossing lightly, until the cheese is melted and the pasta is heated through, 1 to 2 minutes. Serve at once.

Penne with Chicken, Tomatoes, and Artichoke Hearts

I*t is easier to slice raw chicken into thin strips when it is partially frozen—30 to 45 minutes in the freezer should do the trick.* ***Makes 4 servings***

1 pound penne rigate or other tube-shaped pasta with ridges
3 skinless, boneless chicken breast halves (about 1 pound)
1 teaspoon salt
¼ teaspoon pepper
⅓ cup extra-virgin olive oil
½ cup chicken broth
¼ cup fresh lemon juice

4 large garlic cloves, thinly sliced
1 (9-ounce) package frozen artichoke hearts (halves and quarters)
1 pound (about 2 cups) red or yellow cherry tomatoes, halved
1 tablespoon chopped fresh tarragon or ¾ teaspoon dried
⅓ cup grated Parmesan cheese

1) In a large pot of boiling salted water, cook the pasta until tender but still firm, 10 to 12 minutes. Rinse and drain well.

2) Rinse the chicken under cold running water and pat dry. Cut the chicken into thin strips and season with ½ teaspoon of the salt and the pepper.

3) In the same pot, heat 2 tablespoons of the olive oil over medium heat. Add the chicken and cook, stirring, until white throughout but still juicy, 3 to 5 minutes. Remove the chicken and set aside.

4) Add the remaining olive oil, the remaining ½ teaspoon salt, the chicken broth, lemon juice, and garlic to the pot and bring to a boil over medium-high heat. Add the frozen artichoke hearts, cover, and reduce the heat to medium-low. Simmer until the artichoke hearts are just tender, about 5 minutes. Uncover and cook 1 minute longer.

5) Reduce the heat to low and stir in the pasta, chicken, tomatoes, and tarragon. Cook, tossing, until heated through, 1 to 2 minutes. Add the grated Parmesan cheese and toss again. Serve at once.

Rigatoni with Creamy Corn Sauce

Even when made with frozen corn, this rich pasta reminds me of summer. Serve with a crisp white wine and a salad of tender young greens. **Makes 4 servings**

1 pound rigatoni
3 skinless, boneless chicken
  breast halves (about 1 pound)
¾ teaspoon salt
¼ teaspoon pepper
2 tablespoons olive oil
1 garlic clove, minced
1 tablespoon unsalted butter
1 cup heavy cream
½ cup chicken broth

3 medium ears of corn, kernels
  removed, or 1½ cups frozen
  corn kernels, thawed
Dash of cayenne
Dash of grated nutmeg
Dash of sugar
1 cup grated Parmesan cheese
  (about 4 ounces)
¼ cup coarsely chopped fresh
  basil, cilantro, or parsley

1) In a large pot of boiling salted water, cook the pasta until tender but still firm, about 10 minutes. Rinse and drain well.

2) Rinse the chicken under cold running water and pat dry. Cut into thin strips and season with ½ teaspoon of the salt and the pepper.

3) In the same pot, heat the olive oil over medium heat. Add the garlic and cook until fragrant, about 30 seconds. Add the chicken and cook, stirring, until white throughout but still juicy, 3 to 5 minutes. Remove the chicken mixture and set aside.

4) Melt the butter in the same pot over medium heat. Add the cream and increase the heat to high. Bring to a boil and cook, stirring occasionally, until thickened and reduced by one-third, 5 to 7 minutes.

5) Reduce the heat to low. Whisk in the chicken broth and cook, stirring occasionally, until heated through, about 3 minutes. Add the corn, cayenne, nutmeg, and sugar and cook 2 minutes longer.

6) Stir in the pasta, chicken, and remaining ¼ teaspoon salt and cook, tossing, until heated through, 1 to 2 minutes. Add ½ cup of the grated Parmesan cheese and the basil and toss again. Serve at once. Pass the remaining cheese at the table.

Rigatoni with Ground Chicken and Eggplant

Eggplant, with its tender creamy pulp, lends a rich Italian accent to bottled spaghetti sauce.

Makes 4 servings

1 medium eggplant (1 to 1¼ pounds)
1 to 2 teaspoons coarse (kosher) salt
1 pound rigatoni
¼ cup olive oil
1 garlic clove, minced
1 pound ground chicken

½ teaspoon salt
⅛ teaspoon crushed hot red pepper
1 (26-ounce) jar chunky spaghetti sauce
Grated Parmesan or Romano cheese

1) Trim off the ends of the eggplant and cut into ¾-inch dice. (There will be 2½ to 3 cups of diced eggplant.) Sprinkle with the coarse salt and layer in a colander to drain for at least 30 minutes or up to 2 hours. Rinse off the eggplant cubes under cold running water and dry well with paper towels, pressing on the eggplant to remove as much moisture as possible.

2) In a large pot of boiling salted water, cook the pasta until tender but still firm, about 10 minutes. Rinse and drain well.

3) In the same pot, heat 2 tablespoons of the olive oil over medium-high heat. Add the garlic, ground chicken, salt, and crushed red pepper and cook, stirring occasionally to break up the meat, until the chicken has lost all trace of pink, about 7 minutes. Remove the chicken mixture with a slotted spoon.

4) Heat the remaining 2 tablespoons olive oil in the same pot over medium-high heat. Add the eggplant cubes and cook, stirring, until softened and beginning to brown, about 5 minutes. Stir in the spaghetti sauce and cook, stirring occasionally, until heated through, 2 to 3 minutes.

5) Reduce the heat to low. Add the pasta and cook, tossing lightly, until heated through, 1 to 2 minutes. Serve at once. Pass a bowl of grated Parmesan cheese at the table.

Rotelle with Chicken and Roasted Red Bell Pepper Pesto

Rotelle, commonly known as *"wagon wheels," are a great way to capture the robust flavor of this pesto. Adding ingredients such as drained capers, olives, or chopped fresh herbs makes a tasty variation.* **Makes 4 servings**

1 pound rotelle
1 (7.25-ounce) jar roasted red bell peppers, juices reserved
2 to 3 garlic cloves, minced
¼ cup grated Parmesan cheese
¾ teaspoon salt
Dash of cayenne

6 tablespoons extra-virgin olive oil
3 skinless, boneless chicken breast halves (about 1 pound)
¼ teaspoon pepper
Grated Parmesan cheese

1) In a large pot of boiling salted water, cook the pasta until tender but still firm, about 10 minutes. Rinse and drain well.

2) To make the roasted red bell pepper pesto, combine the roasted red bell peppers with their juices, garlic, Parmesan cheese, ¼ teaspoon of the salt, and the cayenne in a food processor or blender. Process until a coarse paste forms. With the machine on, gradually add ¼ cup of the olive oil.

3) Rinse the chicken under cold running water and pat dry. Cut into ¾-inch pieces and season with the remaining ½ teaspoon salt and the pepper.

4) In the same large pot, heat the remaining 2 tablespoons olive oil over medium heat. Add the chicken and cook, stirring, until white throughout but still juicy, 3 to 4 minutes. Reduce the heat to low. Add the pasta and cook, tossing, until heated through, 1 to 2 minutes. Add the roasted red bell pepper pesto and toss again. Serve at once. Pass a bowl of grated Parmesan cheese at the table.

Spaghetti Western

*C*hipotle chiles, which are dried, smoked jalapeños, can be purchased either as a bottled salsa or packed in 7-ounce cans with adobo sauce. Look for these items in Mexican grocery stores and well-stocked supermarkets.

Makes 4 servings

1 pound spaghetti
3 skinless, boneless chicken
   breast halves (about 1 pound)
1 teaspoon salt
¼ teaspoon pepper
3 tablespoons olive oil
2 garlic cloves, minced
2 Anaheim peppers, seeded and
   finely chopped
2 scallions, thinly sliced

1 (28-ounce) can diced tomatoes,
   drained
1 (10-ounce) package frozen corn
   kernels, thawed
2 to 3 teaspoons mashed canned
   chipotle chiles or chipotle salsa
¼ teaspoon ground cumin
⅓ cup coarsely chopped cilantro
Grated dry Monterey Jack or
   Parmesan cheese

1) In a large pot of boiling salted water, cook the pasta until tender but still firm, about 10 minutes. Rinse and drain well.

2) Rinse the chicken under cold running water and pat dry. Cut into thin strips and season with ½ teaspoon of the salt and the pepper.

3) In the same pot, heat 2 tablespoons of the olive oil over medium heat. Add the garlic and cook until fragrant, about 30 seconds. Add the chicken and cook, stirring, until white throughout, 3 to 5 minutes. Remove to a plate.

4) Heat the remaining 1 tablespoon olive oil in the same pot over medium heat. Add the Anaheim peppers and cook, stirring occasionally, until softened but not browned, 2 to 3 minutes. Stir in the scallions and cook 1 minute.

5) Add the remaining ½ teaspoon salt, the tomatoes, corn, chipotles, and cumin and cook, stirring occasionally, until thickened, about 10 minutes. Reduce the heat to low. Add the pasta, chicken, and cilantro and cook, tossing, until heated through, 1 to 2 minutes. Serve at once. Pass a bowl of grated dry Monterey Jack cheese at the table.

Spaghettini with Chicken, Peppers, and Olives

T*hese zesty Italian flavors come together easily, making a colorful and satisfying meal.*

Makes 4 servings

1 pound spaghettini
3 skinless, boneless chicken
   breast halves (about 1 pound)
½ teaspoon salt
¼ teaspoon pepper
¼ cup olive oil
2 garlic cloves, minced
1 (7.25-ounce) jar roasted red bell
   peppers, drained and chopped
   into ½-inch pieces

½ cup oil-cured black olives,
   pitted
3 tablespoons chopped parsley
2 tablespoons drained capers
⅛ teaspoon crushed hot red
   pepper
1 cup grated Romano cheese
   (about 4 ounces)

1) In a large pot of boiling salted water, cook the pasta until tender but still firm, 6 to 8 minutes. Rinse and drain well.

2) Rinse the chicken under cold running water and pat dry. Cut into ¾-inch pieces and season with the salt and pepper.

3) In the same pot, heat the olive oil over medium heat. Add the garlic and cook until fragrant, about 30 seconds. Add the chicken and cook, stirring, until lightly browned on the outside and white throughout, 3 to 4 minutes.

4) Reduce the heat to low. Stir in the roasted peppers, olives, parsley, capers, and crushed red pepper. Add the pasta and cook, tossing, until heated through, 1 to 2 minutes. Add ½ cup grated Romano cheese and toss again. Serve at once. Pass the remaining cheese at the table.

Tortellini with Chicken and Broccoli al Pesto

When paired with a crusty loaf of
bread, small portions of this green garlicky mélange make a
satisfying meal. All that is then needed is fresh fruit for dessert.

Makes 4 servings

2 tablespoons pine nuts (pignoli)
1 bunch of broccoli (about 1
  pound), cut into florets and
  ½-inch pieces (about 3 cups)
1 (9-ounce) package chicken- or
  cheese-filled tortellini
3 skinless, boneless chicken
  breast halves (about 1 pound)

½ teaspoon salt
¼ teaspoon pepper
2 tablespoons olive oil
1 tablespoon unsalted butter
¾ cup pesto sauce, purchased or
  homemade (page 138)
Grated Parmesan cheese

1) In a large dry pot, toast the pine nuts over medium heat, stirring
constantly, until lightly browned, 2 to 4 minutes. Remove the pine nuts from the
pan and set aside to cool.

2) In the same pot, bring lightly salted water to a boil. Add the broccoli
and cook until crisp-tender, 3 to 5 minutes. Remove with a slotted spoon and
drain in a colander.

3) Return the water to a boil over high heat. Add the tortellini and cook
according to package directions. Rinse and drain well.

4) Rinse the chicken under cold running water and pat dry. Cut into
¾-inch pieces and season with the salt and pepper.

5) In the same pot, heat the olive oil over medium heat. Add the chicken
and cook, stirring, until white throughout but still juicy, 3 to 4 minutes.

6) Reduce the heat to low and melt the butter in the same pot. Add the
broccoli and tortellini and cook, tossing, until heated through, 1 to 2 minutes.
Remove the pot from the heat, stir in the pesto, and toss again. Garnish with the
pine nuts and serve at once. Pass a bowl of grated Parmesan cheese at the
table.

Chicken in a Soup Pot

Even though some of our mothers never made *real* soup, the sumptuous aroma of a flavorful broth simmering on top of the stove always smells like home. The ideal pot for soup making is tall and narrow, with a heavy bottom to prevent burning. This could be the same pot you use for boiling pasta, and a Dutch oven will even do in a pinch.

In this chapter you'll learn to make Homemade Chicken Broth, the base for so many soups, sauces, and other recipes throughout this book. I always keep canned chicken broth in my pantry for emergencies, but homemade is infinitely tastier and less expensive.

Satisfy your basic instincts with the stewlike Pasta e

Fagioli, take a trip down memory lane with Chicken-and-Vegetable Noodle Soup. Enjoy the international flavors of Pozole Pronto and Tuscan White Bean Soup with Chicken and Rosemary.

You may be surprised at just how simple making homemade soup can be. And as we all know, there's no soup like chicken soup.

Homemade Chicken Broth

*C*anned chicken broth can be a lifesaver for last-minute meals, but nothing compares to the intense chicken flavor of homemade broth. Best of all, it's fat- and salt-free. For convenience, I like to save the finished broth in one- and two-cup containers. These can be refrigerated for up to three days or frozen for up to three months. **Makes about 10 cups**

3 pounds chicken parts, including backs, necks, wings, and giblets (not livers)
1 large onion, skin left on, cut in half and each half stuck with a clove
2 medium carrots, thickly sliced
1 celery rib with leaves, cut in half crosswise
1 large garlic clove, skin left on, smashed

6 parsley stems without leaves
2 fresh thyme sprigs or ½ teaspoon dried thyme
1 strip of fresh lemon peel, about ¾ inch wide and 2 inches long
½ teaspoon whole black peppercorns
1 small bay leaf

1) Rinse the chicken parts well under cold running water. Place them in a 6- to 8-quart stockpot or soup pot and add enough cold water to cover by 1 inch. Bring to a boil over medium heat, skimming off the foam as it rises to the top.

2) Add all the remaining ingredients, reduce the heat to medium-low, and simmer, partially covered, 2 hours.

3) Strain the broth through a fine-mesh sieve and discard the solids. Let the broth cool to room temperature, then refrigerate until well chilled, at least 4 hours or as long as 3 days. Remove the congealed fat from the top of the broth and discard. If not using the broth within 3 days, freeze in tightly covered containers.

Easy Poached Chicken Breasts

When moist cooked chicken is needed for other recipes, this technique is as easy as it gets. Poached chicken breasts also make a lovely light meal, served with or without the broth. If you have any small pieces of onion, celery, or carrot in your refrigerator, add them to the poaching liquid for extra flavor.

Makes about 4 cups poached chicken meat

4 skinless, boneless chicken breast halves (about 1½ pounds)

1½ cups cold chicken broth or water

1) Trim any fat and gristle from the chicken. Rinse with cold water and place in a small soup pot or large saucepan. Add enough chicken broth to cover by at least ½ inch and bring to a simmer over medium heat. Reduce the heat to low and cook, partially covered, until the chicken is white throughout but still juicy, about 12 minutes.

2) Remove from the heat and let stand in the hot broth, uncovered, 10 minutes longer. (If the chicken will not be used at once, let it cool completely in the broth. Refrigerate the chicken in its broth for up to 2 days.)

3) If using the chicken for a one-pot supper, transfer to a plate. When cool enough to handle, chop or shred the meat as indicated in the recipe. Strain the broth through a fine-mesh sieve and save for other uses.

Poached Chicken-in-a-Pot

A *simple boiled dinner served with mustard or horseradish sauce can be a very comforting thing. And when cooked chicken is needed for salads, sandwiches, or a casserole, this method not only delivers very moist meat, it also provides the added bonus of poached vegetables and chicken broth.*

Yields about 3 cups poached chicken meat. Makes 4 servings

1 (3½-pound) chicken
4 small white turnips (about
   1 pound), peeled and quartered
4 medium carrots, peeled and cut
   diagonally into slices ½ inch
   thick
4 medium celery ribs, cut
   diagonally into slices ½ inch
   thick

2 medium onions, cut into slices
   ½ inch thick
1 large garlic clove, smashed
1 bay leaf
Salt
2 tablespoons chopped parsley

1) Rinse the chicken inside and out under cold running water. Place in a 6- to 8-quart stockpot or soup pot and add enough cold water to cover by 1 inch. Bring to a boil over medium heat, skimming off the foam as it rises to the top.

2) Add the turnips, carrots, celery, onions, garlic, and bay leaf. Reduce the heat to low and simmer, partially covered, until the vegetables are tender and the chicken is white throughout, about 45 minutes.

3) Remove the chicken from the pot and carve or cut into serving pieces; discard the skin. Place the chicken on a warm serving platter and surround with the vegetables. Remove and discard the bay leaf. Skim the fat from the top of the broth; strain the broth through a fine-mesh sieve, discarding the solids. Spoon some of the broth over the chicken and the vegetables. Save the remaining broth for another use. Season to taste with salt. Sprinkle the parsley over the chicken and vegetables and serve at once.

Chicken and Barley Soup

When time permits, feel free to double or triple this recipe since it freezes perfectly.

Makes 4 to 6 servings

1 tablespoon olive oil
1 pound ground chicken
1 teaspoon salt
¼ teaspoon pepper
⅛ teaspoon crushed hot red
  pepper
2 medium celery ribs, cut into
  ½-inch dice (about 1 cup)
1 large carrot, peeled and cut into
  ½-inch dice (about 1 cup)

1 cup coarsely chopped green
  cabbage
1 medium onion, chopped
2 garlic cloves, minced
6 cups chicken broth
1 (14½-ounce) can stewed
  tomatoes, coarsely chopped
⅓ cup barley
1 tablespoon chopped fresh
  thyme or 1 teaspoon dried

1) In a 4- or 5-quart soup pot or Dutch oven, heat the olive oil over medium-high heat. Add the ground chicken, salt, pepper, and crushed red pepper and cook, stirring to break up the meat, until the chicken has lost all trace of pink, about 7 minutes.

2) Add the celery, carrot, cabbage, onion, and garlic and cook, stirring occasionally, until softened but not browned, 3 to 5 minutes. Drain off any excess fat from the pot.

3) Stir in the chicken broth, tomatoes with their juices, barley, and thyme and bring to a boil. Reduce the heat to low and cook, partially covered, until the barley is tender, 45 minutes to 1 hour.

Black Bean Soup with Chicken and Tomatoes

With a well-stocked freezer and pantry, this earthy soup can be on the table in a matter of minutes. For a particularly appealing presentation, garnish each serving with a dollop of sour cream, a spoonful of prepared salsa, and a sprinkling of fresh cilantro. *Makes 4 servings*

4 skinless, boneless chicken
   thighs (about ¾ pound)
1 teaspoon salt
½ teaspoon pepper
2 tablespoons olive oil
1 medium onion, chopped
2 garlic cloves, minced
½ teaspoon ground cumin

3½ cups chicken broth
2 (16-ounce) cans black beans,
   rinsed and drained
1 (14½-ounce) can Mexican-style
   stewed tomatoes, coarsely
   chopped
1 lime, quartered

1) Rinse the chicken under cold running water and pat dry. Cut into ½-inch pieces and season with ½ teaspoon of the salt and ¼ teaspoon of the pepper.

2) In a large saucepan or 4- to 5-quart Dutch oven, heat the olive oil over medium-high heat. Add the chicken and cook, stirring, until lightly browned on the outside, about 4 minutes.

3) Add the onion and garlic and cook, stirring occasionally, until softened but not browned, 3 to 5 minutes. Stir in the cumin, chicken broth, beans, and tomatoes and bring to a boil.

4) Reduce the heat to low and cook, stirring occasionally and mashing the beans with the back of a spoon, 15 minutes. Season the soup with the remaining ½ teaspoon salt and ¼ teaspoon pepper. Serve hot with lime wedges to squeeze into the soup.

Chunky Chicken Chowder

If you have a big pot and a little time, this recipe can be easily doubled. You'll be sure to want leftovers, as this soup tastes even better reheated.

Makes 4 to 6 servings

2 bacon slices, cut crosswise into
   ½-inch pieces
1 teaspoon olive oil
3 tablespoons unsalted butter
1 large onion, cut into ½-inch dice
2 medium celery ribs, cut into
   ½-inch dice (about 1 cup)
1 large carrot, peeled and cut into
   ½-inch dice (about 1 cup)
3 tablespoons flour
3 cups milk
1¾ cups chicken broth
½ pound white or small red
   potatoes, scrubbed and cut into
   ½-inch dice (about 1½ cups)

2 cups corn kernels, fresh or
   thawed frozen
¾ teaspoon salt
¼ teaspoon pepper
Dash of cayenne
Dash of sugar
2 large chicken breast halves on
   the bone (1 to 1¼ pounds), skin
   and excess fat removed
2 tablespoons chopped chives or
   parsley

1) In a 5- to 6-quart soup pot, cook the bacon in the olive oil over medium heat until browned, 5 to 7 minutes. Remove with a slotted spoon and drain on paper towels.

2) Add the butter to the same pot and melt over medium heat. Add the onion, celery, and carrot and cook, stirring occasionally, until softened but not browned, 6 to 8 minutes.

3) Add the flour and cook, stirring constantly, 1 to 2 minutes without allowing to color. Gradually stir in the milk. Increase the heat to medium-high and bring to a boil, whisking until thickened and smooth. Whisk in the chicken broth and reduce the heat to medium. Add the potatoes and cook 10 minutes.

4) Stir in the corn, salt, pepper, cayenne, and sugar. Add the chicken breasts and cook, partially covered, until white throughout, about 15 minutes. Using tongs, remove the chicken to a clean work surface. When cool enough to handle, pull the chicken meat off the bones and tear into bite-size pieces. Discard the bones.

5) Return the bacon and chicken to the pot and cook until heated through, 3 to 4 minutes. Season with additional salt and pepper to taste. Ladle the soup into warm bowls and sprinkle with the chives.

Tuscan White Bean Soup with Chicken and Rosemary

F*lavors reminiscent of Italy transform this economical bean soup into a gracious dinner for 4.*

Makes 4 servings

1 (3½-pound) chicken, quartered, skin and excess fat removed
1 medium onion, chopped
1 medium celery rib, chopped
1 medium carrot, peeled and chopped
3 garlic cloves, minced
1 teaspoon salt
¼ teaspoon pepper

1 bay leaf
2 (15-ounce) cans cannellini or other white beans, rinsed and drained
½ cup dry white wine
1½ tablespoons chopped fresh rosemary or 1½ teaspoons dried
Grated Parmesan cheese

1) Rinse the chicken under cold running water. In a 5- or 6-quart soup pot, combine 2 cups water, the chicken, onion, celery, carrot, garlic, salt, pepper, and bay leaf. Bring to a boil over medium heat, skimming off any foam that rises to the top. Reduce the heat to low and cook, partially covered, until the chicken is white throughout, about 45 minutes. Using tongs, remove the chicken to a clean work surface. When cool enough to handle, pull the chicken meat off the bones and tear into bite-size pieces. Discard the bones.

2) Add 3½ cups of water, the beans, wine, and rosemary to the pot and bring to a boil over medium heat. Reduce the heat to low and cook, stirring occasionally and mashing the beans with the back of a spoon, 10 to 15 minutes. Remove and discard the bay leaf. Season with additional salt and pepper to taste, if desired. Pass a bowl of grated Parmesan cheese at the table.

Pozole Pronto

T*raditional Mexican pozoles are chock-full of everything from hominy (puffed corn kernels) to a pig's head and feet. This simplified version contains only chicken meat—no heads or feet. Be sure your menu includes warm flour tortillas and a colorful assortment of the salad-type garnishes.*

Makes 4 servings

3 skinless, boneless chicken
   breast halves (about 1 pound)
½ teaspoon salt
¼ teaspoon pepper
6 cups chicken broth
1 medium onion, finely chopped
2 garlic cloves, minced
1 (29-ounce) can white hominy,
   rinsed and drained
1½ teaspoons chopped fresh
   oregano or ½ teaspoon dried

2 cups shredded iceberg lettuce
8 radishes, thinly sliced
4 scallions, thinly sliced
4 jalapeño or serrano peppers,
   thinly sliced into rings
1 avocado, peeled and cut into
   ½-inch dice
2 limes, quartered

1) Rinse the chicken under cold running water and cut into ½-inch pieces. Season with the salt and pepper.

2) In a 5- or 6-quart soup pot, bring the chicken broth to a boil over high heat. Add the onion and garlic. Reduce the heat to medium-low and cook until the vegetables are softened, about 7 minutes.

3) Add the hominy and cook until heated through, about 5 minutes. Add the chicken and oregano and cook until the chicken is white throughout but still juicy, about 7 minutes. Season with additional salt and pepper to taste.

4) To serve, place the lettuce, radishes, scallions, jalapeño peppers, avocado, and lime quarters in separate small bowls. Divide the hot soup among 4 warm soup bowls. Pass the garnishes for each diner to add at the table.

Lentil and Chicken Soup

What this soup may lack in beauty, it makes up for in flavor. Add the "cosmetic cloud" of sour cream at the end and no one will be the wiser.

Makes 4 to 6 servings

1 (3½-pound) chicken, quartered and skin and excess fat removed
1 medium onion, chopped
3 medium carrots, peeled and chopped
2 medium celery ribs, chopped
1 teaspoon salt
¼ teaspoon pepper
1 garlic clove, minced

1 bay leaf
1½ cups dried lentils, picked over and rinsed
1 to 2 teaspoons balsamic or sherry wine vinegar, to taste
½ cup sour cream or plain yogurt
¼ cup coarsely chopped cilantro or Italian flat-leaf parsley

1) Rinse the chicken under cold running water. In a 5- or 6-quart soup pot, combine the chicken, 2 cups water, the onion, carrots, celery, salt, pepper, garlic, and bay leaf. Bring to a boil over medium heat, skimming off any foam that rises to the top. Reduce the heat to low and cook, partially covered, until the chicken is white throughout, about 45 minutes. Using tongs, remove the chicken to a clean work surface. When cool enough to handle, pull the chicken meat off the bones and tear into bite-size pieces. Discard the bones.

2) Add 4 cups of water to the pot and bring to a boil over medium-high heat. Add the lentils, reduce the heat to low, and cook, partially covered, until the lentils are tender but still hold their shape, about 35 minutes. Stir in the chicken and cook until heated through, 3 to 4 minutes. Remove and discard the bay leaf. Season the soup with the vinegar and additional salt and pepper to taste.

3) Ladle the soup into warm bowls and top each serving with a dollop of sour cream. Swirl the cream into the soup and sprinkle with the cilantro. Serve at once.

Chicken Soup with Many Little Meatballs

Since the miniature meatballs in this soup delight both children and adults, by all means use this as a bargaining point to recruit help in making them. I happen to have a sentimental spot in my heart for alphabet-shaped pasta, but you can also use orzo (rice-shaped pasta), tiny stars, or any other pastina.   ***Makes 4 servings***

¾ cup fresh bread crumbs
3 tablespoons milk
¾ cup grated Parmesan cheese
   (about 3 ounces)
½ pound ground chicken
1 tablespoon finely chopped
   onion
1 garlic clove, minced
½ teaspoon salt
¼ teaspoon dried thyme

⅛ teaspoon grated nutmeg
8 cups chicken broth
2 medium celery ribs, cut into
   ½-inch dice (about 1 cup)
1 large carrot, peeled and cut into
   ½-inch dice (about 1 cup)
⅓ cup alphabet pasta or other
   pastina
2 tablespoons chopped parsley
Pepper

1) In a medium bowl, combine the bread crumbs and milk. Let stand 5 minutes to soften. Add ¼ cup of the grated Parmesan cheese, the ground chicken, onion, garlic, salt, thyme, and nutmeg and mix until well blended. Shape teaspoonfuls of the meat mixture into tiny meatballs no larger than ¾ inch in diameter.

2) In a 5-quart soup pot, bring the chicken broth to a boil over medium heat. Add the celery, carrot, and pasta and cook until just tender, about 10 minutes.

3) Reduce the heat to low. Add the meatballs and cook, partially covered, until they are cooked through and show no trace of pink, 8 to 10 minutes. Ladle the soup into warm bowls and sprinkle with the parsley. Pass the remaining Parmesan cheese and a peppermill at the table.

Chicken-and-Vegetable Noodle Soup

As a child I loved canned chicken noodle soup—so haute cuisine, yet so safe. And most importantly, those slithery noodles were fun to eat. Although this version is heartier, healthier, and more flavorful, it's still magical.

Makes 4 to 6 servings

8 cups chicken broth
2 large chicken breast halves on the bone (1 to 1¼ pounds), skin and excess fat removed
1 (10-ounce) package frozen peas
2 medium celery ribs, cut into ¼-inch dice
1 large carrot, peeled and cut into ¼-inch dice

1 small onion, finely chopped
6 ounces thin or medium egg noodles
½ teaspoon salt
¼ teaspoon pepper
Chopped parsley

1) In a 5- or 6-quart soup pot, bring the chicken broth to a boil over medium heat. Rinse the chicken breasts under cold running water and carefully add to the broth. Cook, partially covered, until the chicken is white throughout, about 15 minutes. Using tongs, remove the chicken to a clean work surface. When cool enough to handle, pull the chicken meat off the bones and tear into about 1-inch pieces. Discard the bones.

2) Return the chicken broth to a boil over medium heat. Add the frozen peas, celery, carrot, and onion. Return to a boil and add the noodles. Cook, stirring occasionally to break up the peas, until both the noodles and the vegetables are tender, about 10 minutes. Reduce the heat to low. Return the chicken to the pot and simmer until heated through, 1 to 2 minutes. Season with the salt and pepper. Ladle the soup into warm bowls and sprinkle with the parsley.

Chicken Soup with Pasta and Peas

T**his delicate soup is Italian by nature, especially when topped with grated Parmesan cheese. For an Asian flavor, omit the cheese and season with soy sauce instead of salt.*   ***Makes 6 to 8 servings

3 skinless, boneless chicken
   breast halves (about 1 pound)
½ teaspoon salt
¼ teaspoon coarsely ground
   pepper
10 cups chicken broth
8 ounces capelli d'angelo or
   vermicelli

1 (10-ounce) package frozen peas,
   thawed
2 medium carrots, peeled and
   coarsely shredded
2 scallions, cut diagonally into
   slices ½ inch thick
Grated Parmesan cheese

1) Rinse the chicken under cold running water and cut into ½-inch pieces. Season with the salt and pepper.

2) In a 5- or 6-quart soup pot, bring the chicken broth to a boil over high heat. Break the pasta strands into 2 or 3 pieces and add to the broth.

3) Reduce the heat to medium and stir in the chicken, peas, carrots, and scallions. Cook, stirring to break up the strands of pasta, until the chicken is white throughout but still juicy and the pasta and vegetables are tender but still firm, 5 to 7 minutes. Season with additional salt and pepper to taste. Pass a bowl of grated Parmesan cheese at the table.

Pasta e Fagioli

*T*he *name of this Italian pasta and bean combo is often Americanized to sound like "pasta fazool." Serve this stewlike soup in shallow soup plates.*

Makes 6 to 8 servings

5 skinless, boneless chicken
   thighs (about 1 pound)
1 teaspoon salt
½ teaspoon pepper
2 tablespoons olive oil
1 medium onion, chopped
3 garlic cloves, minced
5 cups chicken broth
8 ounces ditalini (short tubes of
   macaroni) or elbow macaroni

2 (16-ounce) cans kidney beans,
   rinsed and drained
1 (28-ounce) can crushed
   tomatoes with added puree
3 tablespoons chopped parsley
1 tablespoon chopped fresh
   oregano or 1 teaspoon dried
⅛ teaspoon crushed hot red
   pepper
Grated Parmesan cheese

1) Rinse the chicken under cold running water and pat dry. Cut into ½-inch pieces and season with ½ teaspoon of the salt and ¼ teaspoon of the pepper.

2) In a 5-quart soup pot or Dutch oven, heat the olive oil over medium-high heat. Add the chicken and cook, stirring, until lightly browned on the outside, about 4 minutes. Remove with a slotted spoon and set aside.

3) Reduce the heat to medium. Add the onion and garlic to the pot and cook, stirring occasionally, until softened but not browned, 3 to 5 minutes. Add the chicken broth and bring to a boil.

4) Stir in the pasta and reduce the heat to low. Cook until the pasta is tender but still firm, 10 to 15 minutes. Add the chicken, beans, tomatoes with their puree, parsley, oregano, and hot red pepper. Cook, stirring occasionally, until heated through, 5 to 7 minutes. Season the soup with the remaining ½ teaspoon salt and ¼ teaspoon pepper to taste. Pass a bowl of grated Parmesan cheese at the table.

Cheesy Chicken Soup with Herbed Polenta

With its heavenly aroma and creamy texture, this hearty soup soothes the soul. Serve with a crisp green salad and a crusty loaf of bread. ***Makes 4 servings***

1 (3½-pound) chicken, quartered and skin and excess fat removed
1 (14½-ounce) can diced tomatoes, drained
1 medium onion, finely chopped
1 large garlic clove, minced
1 teaspoon salt
½ teaspoon coarsely ground pepper

⅛ teaspoon crushed hot red pepper
¾ cup instant polenta or yellow cornmeal
3 tablespoons coarsely chopped basil, mint, or parsley
½ cup shredded Fontina or mozzarella cheese (about 2 ounces)

1) Rinse the chicken under cold running water. In a 5- or 6-quart soup pot, combine 2 cups water, the chicken, tomatoes, onion, garlic, ½ teaspoon of the salt, the pepper, and hot pepper. Bring to a boil over medium heat, skimming off any foam that rises to the top. Reduce the heat to low and cook, partially covered, until the chicken is white throughout, about 45 minutes.

2) Using tongs, remove the chicken to a clean work surface. When cool enough to handle, pull the chicken meat off the bones and tear into bite-size pieces. Discard the bones.

3) Meanwhile, add 4 cups of water to the pot and bring to a boil over medium-high heat. Whisk in the polenta in a slow, steady stream. Reduce the heat to medium-low and cook, stirring often, until the mixture has thickened and the polenta is creamy to the bite, about 7 minutes. Stir in the chicken, basil, and the remaining ½ teaspoon salt and cook until heated through, 1 to 2 minutes.

4) Ladle the soup into 4 warm bowls. Top each with 2 tablespoons of the shredded Fontina cheese and serve at once.

South-of-the-Border
Chicken Soup

This fragrant soup is loaded with chunks of chicken and fresh vegetables. Serve with warm flour tortillas or bread.

Makes 4 servings

3 skinless, boneless chicken
   breast halves (about 1 pound)
6 cups chicken broth
1 small onion, chopped
1 teaspoon dried oregano
1 teaspoon ground cumin
2 garlic cloves, minced
½ teaspoon salt
¼ teaspoon pepper

1 bay leaf
3 medium carrots, peeled and cut
   into ½-inch dice
1 (15-ounce) can garbanzo beans,
   rinsed and drained
1 medium zucchini, cut into
   ½-inch dice
¼ cup coarsely chopped cilantro

1) Rinse the chicken under cold running water and cut into ½-inch pieces.

2) In a 5-quart soup pot, combine the chicken broth, onion, oregano, cumin, garlic, salt, pepper, and bay leaf. Bring to a boil over high heat.

3) Reduce the heat to low and stir in the carrots and garbanzo beans. Cook until the carrots are softened, about 7 minutes. Stir in the chicken and zucchini and cook until the chicken is white throughout and the zucchini is tender, about 7 minutes longer. Remove and discard the bay leaf. Stir in the cilantro and season with additional salt and pepper to taste.

Chicken Soup with Tortellini and Spinach

*T*his tasty soup goes together very quickly and benefits from the addition of fresh vegetables. One can't help but think that if Popeye were Italian, this would be his favorite.

Makes 4 servings

4 skinless, boneless chicken
  thighs (about ¾ pound)
1 teaspoon salt
¼ teaspoon pepper
2 tablespoons olive oil
3 medium carrots, peeled and
  chopped
1 medium onion, chopped

2 garlic cloves, minced
4 cups chicken broth
1 bunch of fresh spinach (about
  1 pound), washed, drained, and
  coarsely chopped
1 (9-ounce) package cheese-filled
  tortellini
Grated Parmesan cheese

1) Rinse the chicken under cold running water and pat dry. Cut into ½-inch pieces and season with ½ teaspoon of the salt and the pepper.

2) In a 5-quart soup pot or Dutch oven, heat the olive oil over medium-high heat. Add the chicken and cook, stirring, until lightly browned on the outside, about 4 minutes.

3) Add the carrots, onion, and garlic and cook, stirring occasionally, until softened but not browned, 3 to 5 minutes.

4) Add the chicken broth and bring to a boil. Stir in the spinach and tortellini. Reduce the heat to medium and cook as the tortellini package directs, anywhere from 5 to 9 minutes. Season with the remaining ½ teaspoon salt. Pass a bowl of grated Parmesan cheese at the table.

Chicken with Indian-Spiced Rice and Vegetables

This colorful supper, with its heady aroma and exotic flavors, is ideal for casual entertaining. Serve with your favorite fruit chutney and iced glasses of cold beer.

Makes 4 servings

10 chicken thighs on the bone
   (about 2½ pounds)
2 teaspoons salt
2 tablespoons vegetable oil
3 medium onions, chopped
2 tablespoons grated fresh ginger
1 tablespoon ground coriander
4 garlic cloves, minced
¼ to ½ teaspoon cayenne, to taste

2 cups chicken broth
1 (15-ounce) can garbanzo beans,
   rinsed and drained
1 (14½-ounce) can diced
   tomatoes, drained
1 (9-ounce) package frozen cut
   green beans, thawed
1 cup basmati or long-grain white
   rice

1) Preheat oven to 400 degrees F. Rinse the chicken with cold water and pat dry. Remove and discard the skin and any visible fat. Season with 1 teaspoon of the salt. In a large flameproof casserole, heat 1 tablespoon of the oil over medium-high heat until hot. Add the chicken, in batches if necessary, and cook, turning, until browned all over, 8 to 10 minutes. Remove the chicken to a plate.

2) Reduce the heat to low. Add the remaining 1 tablespoon oil and heat until hot. Add the onions and cook, stirring occasionally, until golden, 10 to 12 minutes. Add the ginger, coriander, garlic, and cayenne. Cook, stirring, until fragrant, about 2 minutes.

3) Increase the heat to medium-high. Add the chicken broth, garbanzo beans, tomatoes, green beans, and remaining 1 teaspoon salt. Return the chicken to the pot, cover, and bake until the rice is tender and most of the liquid has been absorbed, 20 to 25 minutes.

Chicken Supper in the Oven

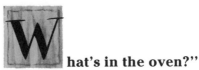

What's in the oven?''
Anyone who has ever spent more than 15 minutes in a kitchen during his or her lifetime has surely been asked that question. This chapter will give you some new answers:

"Well, there's a Baked Chicken Salad with a new twist for the Nineties."

"There's a Terrific Tamale Pie!"

"You're going to *love* the Summer Chicken and Tomato Gratin with Fresh Basil."

"One of my very favorite quickies, Pollo Express."

"Uncork the Chianti! Tonight it's Cheesy Chicken Breasts Marinara."

And, "Can't you smell the Crispy Roast Chicken with Pan-Roasted Vegetables?"

The cooking equipment required for these recipes is nothing out of the ordinary; it might be a casserole, gratin dish, roasting pan, or even a baking sheet. Many of these can go right from oven to table. There is an endless supply of reasonably priced, good-looking bakeware on the market—I tend to favor the ovenproof oval clear glass gratin dishes that are widely available. Casserole dishes range from utilitarian to envy-inducing—just take a stroll through the housewares section of your local department store.

You'll notice that a number of the recipes in this chapter call for shredded or chopped cooked chicken. Since one-pot meals stress ease of preparation, a take-out rotisserie chicken is a great resource. If you happen to have on hand some leftover Easy Poached Chicken Breasts from page 112, that meat would be ideal for any of these dishes.

Since many of these meals can be prepared in advance, a lot of your future standbys for both weeknight dinners and entertaining will probably come from this chapter. So preheat the oven—it's time to get started!

Chile Chicken Squares

This versatile combo is a hit at breakfast, lunch, or dinner. In fact, it can even be cut into smaller squares for appetizers.

Makes 4 to 6 servings

4 tablespoons unsalted butter
5 eggs
¼ cup flour
½ teaspoon baking powder
⅛ teaspoon salt
Dash of cayenne
2 cups shredded Monterey Jack or
   Cheddar cheese (about 8
   ounces)

1 cup small-curd cottage cheese
1 (4-ounce) can diced green chiles
1½ cups chopped or shredded
   cooked chicken

1) Preheat the oven to 400 degrees F. Melt the butter in a 9-inch-square baking dish in the oven. Tip the baking dish to evenly coat the bottom and sides with the butter.

2) In a large bowl, whisk the eggs until well blended. Stir in the flour, baking powder, salt, and cayenne. Pour the butter from the baking dish into the egg mixture. Add the Monterey Jack cheese, cottage cheese, and chiles and blend well.

3) Spread the chicken evenly in the buttered dish. Pour the egg mixture over the chicken and bake 15 minutes. Reduce the oven temperature to 350 degrees and bake until the top is lightly browned and a knife inserted in the center shows no evidence of uncooked egg, 30 to 35 minutes.

4) Let cool on a rack at least 10 minutes. Cut into squares to serve. (If made in advance, cover and refrigerate up to 2 days. Freeze for longer storage.) Serve warm or at room temperature.

Pollo Express

If you assemble this in advance and refrigerate it, allow about 10 minutes extra time for baking. Serve this crowd-pleasing casserole with warm flour tortillas and a crisp green salad. **Makes 6 servings**

4 cups coarsely shredded cooked chicken
1 (15-ounce) can chili without beans
1 (11-ounce) can corn kernels, drained
1 bunch of scallions, coarsely chopped (about 1 cup)
1 (7-ounce) can green chile salsa
1 (2¼-ounce) can sliced pitted ripe olives, drained

1 (3-ounce) package cream cheese, cut into bits
½ teaspoon salt
1 cup shredded Cheddar cheese (about 4 ounces)
1 cup shredded Monterey Jack cheese (about 4 ounces)
Cilantro sprigs and sour cream

1) Preheat the oven to 350 degrees F. Spread the chicken evenly into a greased 14-inch oval gratin or other large shallow baking dish.

2) In a large bowl, combine the chili, corn, scallions, salsa, olives, cream cheese, and salt. Mix well. Pour the mixture over the chicken and top with the shredded cheeses. (The recipe can be prepared to this point up to a day in advance. Cover and refrigerate.)

3) Bake, uncovered, until heated through and bubbly, about 30 minutes. Garnish with the cilantro sprigs. Pass the sour cream at the table.

Baked Chicken Breasts with Corn Bread Dressing

With the help of several
convenience foods, this zesty dinner goes together in minutes.

Makes 4 servings

¾ cup chicken broth or water
2 tablespoons unsalted butter, cut
    into 8 pieces
1 (6-ounce) bag seasoned corn
    bread stuffing mix (about
    2 cups)
1 cup frozen corn kernels, thawed
¾ cup mild salsa
1 (2¼-ounce) can sliced pitted
    ripe olives, drained

4 skinless, boneless chicken
    breast halves (about
    1½ pounds)
½ teaspoon salt
¼ teaspoon pepper
½ cup shredded Cheddar or
    Monterey Jack cheese (about
    2 ounces)
2 tablespoons chopped cilantro or
    parsley

1) Preheat the oven to 350 degrees F. Combine the chicken broth and butter in a 12x8-inch baking dish and place in the oven. Heat until the broth is hot and the butter has melted, 2 to 3 minutes. Remove from the oven. Stir in the stuffing mix, corn, ¼ cup of the salsa, and the olives. Mix well.

2) Rinse the chicken under cold running water and pat dry. Season with the salt and pepper.

3) Arrange the chicken breasts in a single layer over the stuffing and top with the remaining ½ cup salsa. Cover and bake until the chicken is white throughout but still juicy, about 30 minutes.

4) Sprinkle 2 tablespoons of the cheese over each chicken breast. Bake, uncovered, until the cheese has melted, about 5 minutes longer. Top with the cilantro just before serving.

Layered Enchilada Casserole

For a particularly attractive
presentation, top each serving with a shower of shredded lettuce and
a few slices of pickled jalapeño pepper.   ***Makes 6 servings***

1 (28-ounce) can crushed
  tomatoes with added puree
2 teaspoons chili powder
½ teaspoon ground cumin
12 (6- or 7-inch) corn tortillas
3 cups shredded cooked chicken
2 cups shredded Monterey Jack or
  Cheddar cheese (about 8
  ounces)

1½ cups sour cream, whisked
  until smooth
1 (7-ounce) can diced green chiles
3 scallions, chopped
1 (2¼-ounce) can pitted ripe olive
  slices, drained

1) Preheat the oven to 350 degrees F. In a medium bowl, mix the tomatoes
and their puree with the chili powder and cumin until well blended. In a
14-inch oval gratin or other shallow baking dish, place 4 tortillas, overlapping as
necessary to cover the bottom of the dish. Layer one-third each of the tomato
mixture, chicken, cheese, sour cream, chiles, scallions, and olives over the
tortillas.

2) Top with 4 more tortillas and a layer of half of the remaining tomato
mixture, chicken, cheese, sour cream, chiles, scallions and olives. Repeat the
layers of the tortillas, chicken, sour cream, chiles, scallions, and olives once
more. Cover with the tomato mixture and the cheese. (The recipe can be
prepared to this point up to a day in advance. Cover and refrigerate.)

3) Bake, uncovered, until the edges are bubbly hot and the casserole is
heated through, about 30 minutes.

Cheesy Chicken Breasts Marinara

This dish can be dressed up by adding ingredients such as sautéed mushrooms or eggplant or by serving it over pasta. But when time or imagination runs short, garlic bread and a crisp green salad are all that is really needed for a great dinner. ***Makes 4 servings***

4 skinless, boneless chicken
   breast halves (about
   1½ pounds)
½ teaspoon salt
¼ teaspoon pepper

4 ounces mozzarella cheese,
   sliced
1 cup prepared marinara or
   spaghetti sauce
1 tablespoon chopped parsley

1) Preheat the oven to 350 degrees F. Rinse the chicken under cold running water and pat dry. Season with the salt and pepper and arrange in a single layer in a lightly oiled 9-inch-square baking dish.

2) Cover the chicken breasts with cheese slices and pour the marinara sauce over all. Cover and bake until the chicken is white throughout but still juicy, about 30 minutes.

3) Uncover and bake until the sauce is bubbly hot and lightly browned on top, 5 to 10 minutes longer. Garnish with the parsley just before serving.

Barbecued Chicken Pizza

Sounds weird? You bet. But be
forewarned—your guests will come back for seconds.

Makes 4 to 6 servings

1 tablespoon olive oil
2 teaspoons cornmeal
1 (1-pound) loaf frozen bread
  dough, thawed as package
  directs
2 cups chopped or shredded
  cooked chicken
1½ cups barbecue sauce

1 small yellow or green bell
  pepper, cut into ½-inch squares
3 thin slices of red onion, cut in
  half and separated into pieces
3 cups shredded Monterey Jack
  cheese (about 12 ounces)

1) Preheat the oven to 400 degrees F. Coat a 15-inch pizza pan with the
olive oil and sprinkle evenly with the cornmeal. Roll out or stretch the dough to
fit the pan.

2) In a medium bowl, combine the chicken and the barbecue sauce.
Spread the mixture into an even layer over the dough. Scatter the bell pepper
and onion over the top and cover with the shredded cheese.

3) Place the pizza pan on the lowest shelf in an electric oven (or on the
floor of a gas oven) and bake until the crust is firm and nicely browned, 15 to
20 minutes. Cut into wedges and serve warm.

Chicken and Pesto Pizza

*I*f you do not have a pizza pan,
shape the dough on a baking sheet. **Makes 4 to 6 servings**

1 tablespoon olive oil
2 teaspoons cornmeal
1 (1-pound) loaf frozen bread
   dough, thawed as package
   directs
Pesto alla Genovese (recipe
   follows) or ¾ cup pesto,
   purchased or homemade

2 cups chopped cooked chicken
2 tablespoons pine nuts (pignoli)
3 cups shredded mozzarella
   cheese (about 12 ounces)

1) Preheat the oven to 400 degrees F. Coat a 15-inch pizza pan with the olive oil and sprinkle evenly with the cornmeal. Roll out or stretch the dough to fit the pan.

2) Spread the pesto over the dough and top with an even layer of the chicken. Sprinkle with the pine nuts and cover with the shredded cheese.

3) Place the pizza pan on the lowest shelf in an electric oven (or on the floor of a gas oven) and bake until the crust is firm and nicely browned, 15 to 20 minutes. Cut into wedges and serve warm.

Pesto alla Genovese

It seems like pesto is now made from just about any herb that strikes someone's fancy. That's all well and good. Just remember that the prototype for these radical departures is made with the most fragrant herb of all, sweet basil.

Makes about ¾ cup

1 cup (packed) basil leaves
1 garlic clove
¼ cup grated Parmesan cheese

½ teaspoon salt
⅛ teaspoon pepper
¼ cup extra-virgin olive oil

1) In a food processor or blender, combine the basil, garlic, grated Parmesan cheese, salt, and pepper. Process until a coarse paste forms. With the machine on, gradually add the olive oil.

2) Use the pesto immediately, refrigerate in an airtight container for up to 4 days, or freeze.

Oven-Baked Chicken Piccata

Enjoy these popular piquant *flavors without any last-minute fuss.*

Makes 4 servings

1 pound small red or white
  potatoes, cut into slices
  ½ inch thick
1 (9-ounce) package frozen
  artichoke hearts, thawed
6 medium shallots, thinly sliced
3 tablespoons olive oil
1½ teaspoons chopped fresh
  oregano or ½ teaspoon dried

1 teaspoon salt
½ teaspoon pepper
1 (3½-pound) chicken, cut into
  8 pieces
2 lemons, thinly sliced and seeds
  removed
1½ tablespoons drained capers
1 cup dry white wine
2 tablespoons chopped parsley

1) Preheat the oven to 350 degrees F. In a 14-inch oval gratin or other baking dish, toss the potatoes, artichoke hearts, and shallots with 2 tablespoons of the olive oil, the oregano, ½ teaspoon of the salt, and ¼ teaspoon of the pepper until well mixed. Spread the vegetables in a single layer.

2) Rinse the chicken under cold running water. Remove as much skin and excess fat from the chicken as possible and pat dry. Season the chicken with the remaining ½ teaspoon salt and ¼ teaspoon pepper and place in a single layer over the vegetables. Scatter the lemon slices and capers over the top and gently pour the wine over all. Drizzle with the remaining 1 tablespoon olive oil.

3) Bake until the vegetables are tender and the chicken is white throughout but still juicy, 35 to 45 minutes. Garnish with the chopped parsley just before serving.

One-Pot Chicken Potpie

A free-floating crown of puff pastry elevates this homey entrée from delicious to sublime. Use the leftover scraps of pastry for cutting decorations for the crust—the less-than-artistic can rely on cookie cutters for the job.

Makes 4 to 6 servings

4 skinless, boneless chicken breast halves (about 1½ pounds)
1 stick (4 ounces) unsalted butter
½ cup flour
3½ cups chicken broth
2 medium red or white potatoes (about ¾ pound), scrubbed and cut into ½-inch dice
1 medium onion, cut into ½-inch dice
¼ pound medium mushrooms, quartered
1 large celery rib, cut into ½-inch dice

1 large carrot, peeled and cut into ½-inch dice
1½ teaspoons chopped fresh thyme or ½ teaspoon dried
1 teaspoon salt
½ teaspoon pepper
½ cup frozen peas, thawed
2 tablespoons chopped parsley
1 sheet frozen puff pastry (half of a 17¼-ounce package), thawed in the refrigerator
1 egg yolk
1 tablespoon milk

1) Preheat the oven to 350 degrees F. Rinse the chicken under cold running water and pat dry. Cut into ¾-inch pieces.

2) In a 3-inch-deep, 12-inch-round ovenproof skillet or flameproof casserole, melt the butter over medium heat. Add the flour and cook, stirring constantly, 2 minutes, without allowing to color. Gradually whisk in the chicken broth and cook, whisking constantly, until the sauce boils and thickens, about 2 minutes. Stir in the chicken, potatoes, onion, mushrooms, celery, carrot, thyme, salt, and pepper.

3) Cover and bake 30 minutes. Remove from the oven. Increase the oven temperature to 425 degrees. Stir in the peas and parsley. Season with additional salt and pepper to taste.

4) On a lightly floured work surface, roll the sheet of well-chilled pastry into a 12-inch square, then trim into a round 12 inches in diameter. Lay the pastry round over the filling. Cut several decorative silts in the pastry to vent the steam. In a small bowl, mix the egg yolk and milk until well blended. Brush the glaze over the pastry. Decorate with pastry scraps, if desired, and brush again with the egg yolk mixture.

5) Bake until the crust is puffed and golden and the filling is bubbly hot, about 25 minutes.

Oven-Baked Chicken Quesadillas

*T*hese little grilled cheese *sandwiches are always a hit. This method of preparation also makes them a snap to produce.*

Makes 4 quesadillas

8 (7-inch) flour tortillas
2 tablespoons vegetable oil
1 cup chopped cooked chicken
1 cup shredded Monterey Jack or
  Cheddar cheese (about
  4 ounces)

3 or 4 pickled jalapeño peppers,
  seeded and minced
Fresh cilantro sprigs
Sour cream and salsa

1) Preheat the oven to 500 degrees F. Brush 1 side of each of 4 tortillas with oil and place, oiled side down, on a baking sheet. Evenly distribute ¼ cup each of chicken and cheese over each tortilla. Sprinkle with a few bits of jalapeño pepper. Top with the remaining tortillas, pressing down gently to form sandwiches, and brush with oil. Bake until the cheese is melted and the tortillas are lightly browned, 5 to 7 minutes.

2) Using a large spatula, transfer the quesadillas to a cutting board. Use a pizza wheel or a large sharp knife to cut into wedges. Garnish with the cilantro sprigs. Pass the sour cream and salsa at the table.

Baked Chicken Salad

*T*he familiar tastes of your
*favorite cold chicken salad take on a whole new character when the
salad is served warm. This makes a lovely luncheon dish.*

Makes 4 servings

3 cups coarsely chopped cooked
  chicken
3 medium celery ribs, cut into
  ¼-inch dice
½ cup mayonnaise
⅓ cup sour cream
⅓ cup toasted slivered almonds
1 scallion, chopped
2 oil-packed sun-dried tomato
  halves, drained and finely
  chopped

2 teaspoons chopped fresh
  tarragon or parsley
¼ teaspoon salt
¼ teaspoon pepper
⅛ teaspoon tarragon or other
  white wine vinegar
1 cup shredded Cheddar cheese
  (about 4 ounces)

1) Preheat the oven to 350 degrees F. In a 2-quart baking dish, combine the chicken, celery, mayonnaise, sour cream, almonds, scallion, sun-dried tomatoes, tarragon, salt, pepper, and vinegar until well blended. Top with the shredded cheese.

2) Bake until the mixture is bubbly hot and the cheese has melted, about 30 minutes. Serve at once.

Thighs on a Roll with Rosemary

Italian in spirit but truly unique, this rustic chicken nestled in bread dough smells heavenly as it bakes. Those who do not share my love of spicy foods should opt for the smaller amounts of the red and black peppers. Serve with a salad made from romaine lettuce, crisp cucumber slices, tiny chunks of goat cheese, and good olives.

Makes 4 to 6 servings

8 well-chilled chicken thighs (about 2 pounds), skinned if desired
1 large onion, thinly sliced
3 large garlic cloves, thinly sliced
⅓ cup lemon juice
⅓ cup plus 1 tablespoon extra-virgin olive oil
1 to 2 teaspoons crushed hot red pepper
1 to 2 teaspoons coarsely ground black pepper

2 teaspoons yellow cornmeal
2 (1-pound) loaves frozen bread dough, thawed as package directs
3 tablespoons coarsely chopped fresh rosemary or 1 tablespoon dried
1½ teaspoons coarse (kosher) salt

1) Rinse the chicken under cold running water and pat dry. Place the chicken, onion, and garlic in a heavy-duty 1-gallon plastic food storage bag. Add the lemon juice, ⅓ cup of the olive oil, the crushed red pepper, and black pepper. Seal the bag securely and turn over several times to coat the chicken. Refrigerate at least 4 hours or as long as overnight.

2) Brush a pizza pan or baking sheet with the remaining 1 tablespoon olive oil and sprinkle with the cornmeal. On a lightly floured work surface, place both loaves of bread dough. Sprinkle the dough with 2½ tablespoons of the fresh rosemary or all of the dried and knead together until well mixed. Let the dough rest 5 minutes.

3) Place the dough on the prepared pan and roll or press the dough into a 12-inch circle. Arrange the chicken thighs over the dough, topping with the onion and garlic. (Do not blot the chicken dry; the marinade clinging to the ingredients is needed for flavor.) Let rest in a warm place (75 to 80 degrees F) until the dough is nicely puffed around the chicken pieces, about 1¼ hours. Preheat the oven to 375 degrees F.

4) Sprinkle the chicken with the salt and bake until the dough is golden brown at the edges and the chicken is cooked through, about 45 minutes. Sprinkle the remaining ½ tablespoon fresh rosemary over the top. Cut into wedges and serve warm.

Terrific Tamale Pie

*T*his is great for potlucks or other large gatherings and is usually a big hit with the kids. If made in advance, reheat, partially covered, until warmed through.

Makes 8 to 10 servings

1½ cups yellow cornmeal
1½ cups milk
2 eggs
⅛ teaspoon sugar
Dash of cayenne
3 tablespoons olive oil
1½ pounds ground chicken
1 large onion, chopped
3 garlic cloves, minced
1 tablespoon chili powder

1 teaspoon ground cumin
1 teaspoon dried oregano
½ teaspoon salt
1 (14½-ounce) can Mexican-style stewed tomatoes, drained and chopped
1 (16-ounce) package frozen corn kernels, thawed
1 (2¼-ounce) can sliced pitted ripe olives, drained

1) Preheat the oven to 350 degrees F. In a medium bowl, mix the cornmeal, milk, eggs, sugar, and cayenne until well blended.

2) In a deep 12-inch ovenproof skillet or 3-quart casserole, heat the olive oil over medium-high heat. Add the ground chicken, onion, garlic, chili powder, oregano, and salt and cook, stirring to break up the meat, until the chicken has lost all trace of pink, about 7 minutes. Remove the skillet from the heat and stir in the cornmeal mixture, tomatoes, corn, and olives until well mixed.

3) Bake until lightly browned on top and heated through, about 1½ hours.

Chicken and Sun-Dried Tomato Strata

The versatile strata, a layered casserole of bread and cheese, has long been a standby for entertaining at breakfast, lunch, and dinner. This updated version is a real winner. Just be cautious with the salt and pepper—packaged croutons are often highly seasoned. **Makes 8 to 10 servings**

4 cups large (½- to ¾-inch) croutons, purchased or homemade (6 to 8 ounces)
3 cups coarsely chopped cooked chicken
2 cups shredded mozzarella cheese (about 8 ounces)
1 cup shredded Cheddar or Monterey Jack cheese

½ cup thinly sliced scallions
12 oil-packed sun-dried tomato halves, drained and finely chopped
5 eggs
1½ cups milk
Salt and pepper
⅓ cup grated Parmesan cheese

1) Preheat the oven to 350 degrees F. In a lightly greased 13 x 9-inch baking dish, layer 2 cups of the croutons, 1½ cups of the chicken, 1 cup of the mozzarella cheese, ½ cup of the Cheddar cheese, all of the scallions, and all of the sun-dried tomatoes. Repeat the layers with the remaining 2 cups croutons, 1½ cups chicken, 1 cup mozzarella cheese, and ½ cup Cheddar cheese.

2) In a medium mixing bowl, whisk together the eggs and milk until well blended. If using unseasoned croutons, mix in ¼ teaspoon salt and ¼ teaspoon pepper. Pour the egg mixture into the baking dish, gently patting the croutons down once or twice to moisten with the egg mixture. Sprinkle with the grated Parmesan cheese. (The recipe can be prepared to this point up to 3 hours in advance. Cover and refrigerate.)

3) Bake, uncovered, until the top is nicely browned and a knife inserted into the center shows no evidence of uncooked egg, 30 to 40 minutes. Let stand 30 minutes before cutting into squares to serve.

Crispy Roast Chicken with Pan-Roasted Vegetables

Regardless of the time of year or the day of the week, this is one of my favorite suppers. This chicken is so good on its own that I often roast two at a time in a larger pan so I'll have leftovers for sandwiches, salads, or such dishes as Chicken with Pineapple and Red Bell Pepper (page 55).

Makes 4 servings

1 whole chicken (3½ to 4 pounds)
1 teaspoon salt
¼ teaspoon pepper
1 lemon, cut in half
1 small onion, quartered
2 garlic cloves, smashed
1 large fresh herb sprig, such as
   rosemary, sage, or parsley
½ teaspoon paprika
1 tablespoon olive oil

12 small red potatoes (about
   1 pound)
2 medium onions, peeled and cut
   through the root end into
   6 wedges each
6 carrots (about 1 pound), peeled
   and cut into 1½-inch-thick slices
½ cup dry white wine or chicken
   broth

1) Preheat the oven to 425 degrees F. Remove the chicken neck, giblets, and pockets of fat from the chicken cavity and reserve for other uses. Rinse the chicken inside and out under cold running water and pat dry. Rub the cavity with the salt and pepper. Squeeze the juice from one lemon half over the chicken, then place the remaining lemon skin and pulp, the onion, garlic, and herb sprig in the cavity. Cross the bone ends of the legs and tie together with kitchen string. Sprinkle the chicken with the paprika and rub all over with the olive oil.

2) Place the chicken on a rack in a lightly greased 15 x 12-inch roasting pan. Scatter the vegetables in the bottom of the pan surrounding the chicken. Pour the wine over the vegetables. Roast, turning the vegetables once or twice to coat with the juices, until the vegetables are tender and the chicken is crisp and brown on the outside and white throughout, 45 to 55 minutes. (The juices should run clear when a thigh is pricked with a fork at the thickest point.)

3) Remove the chicken from the oven, cover loosely with foil, and let rest 15 minutes before carving. Using a slotted spoon, remove the vegetables to a serving platter and keep warm. Skim the fat from the pan juices and discard. Just before serving, squeeze the remaining lemon half over the chicken. Serve with the pan juices.

Summer Chicken and Tomato Gratin with Fresh Basil

Make this when your garden is filled with sweet, vine-ripened tomatoes. If you're not a gardener, this is definitely worth a trip to the farmers' market. You'll also want to have some good bread on hand to mop up the sauce.

Makes 4 servings

4 skinless, boneless chicken
  breast halves (about
  1½ pounds)
1 tablespoon lemon juice
1 tablespoon olive oil
1 tablespoon shredded fresh basil
  or chopped parsley
1 teaspoon salt

1 garlic clove, minced
3 large beefsteak tomatoes (about
  1½ pounds), cut into slices
  ½ inch thick
6 tablespoons heavy cream
¼ teaspoon pepper
¼ cup grated Parmesan cheese
Fresh basil sprigs

1) Trim any external fat or gristle from the edges of the chicken. Pound the thicker ends gently with the side of a large knife to flatten evenly. Rinse the chicken under cold running water and pat dry. In a bowl or heavy-duty 1-quart plastic food storage bag, combine the chicken, lemon juice, olive oil, 1 teaspoon of the basil, ½ teaspoon of the salt, and the garlic. Marinate at room temperature 30 minutes.

2) Preheat the oven to 375 degrees F. In a lightly greased 12-inch gratin or other shallow baking dish, arrange the tomato slices, overlapping as necessary to cover the bottom of the dish. Drizzle with the cream and season with the remaining ½ teaspoon salt and the pepper. Scatter the remaining 2 teaspoons basil over the top.

3) Arrange the chicken breasts in a single layer over the tomatoes. Bake until the chicken is white throughout but still juicy, about 25 minutes. Sprinkle with grated Parmesan cheese on top and bake until the cheese has melted, about 5 minutes longer. Garnish with the fresh basil sprigs. Serve warm or at room temperature.

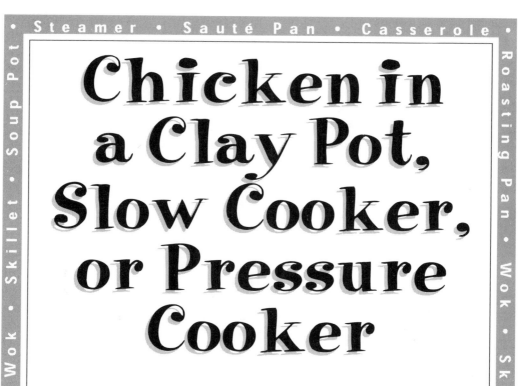

Chicken in a Clay Pot, Slow Cooker, or Pressure Cooker

This chapter contains one-pot chicken recipes developed for cooking equipment you may already have in your kitchen or equipment you may be interested in purchasing. Each has its own distinct merits, which I will describe briefly.

Clay Pots: Cooking in

unglazed terra-cotta wet clay dates back to the ancient Etruscans. Pots are now made in several shapes and sizes by such companies as Romertopf of Germany.

Prior to cooking, the top and bottom of the pot must be soaked in a sinkful of cold water for 15 minutes to saturate the porous clay with water. The uncooked food is then enclosed in the wet covered pot and placed in a cold oven. The oven temperature is set at high heat and, as the food cooks in its own juices without basting and without added fat, the moisture from the sealed clay creates a unique baking environment that produces particularly succulent foods. Keep in mind:

• Clay pots are for oven cooking only. Do not place the pot on an electric or gas burner.

• Avoid sudden temperature changes that could cause the pot to crack; never pour hot liquid into a cold pot or cold liquid into a hot pot. Always place the cold pot in a cold oven. When you remove the pot from the hot oven, place it on a towel or trivet, rather than a cold tile counter, to cool.

• Carefully follow the manufacturer's instructions for cleaning and storage.

Slow Cookers: Electric

crockery cookers are generally known by the brand name Crock-Pot. The concept of this slow, moist-heat method of cooking is straightforward: After minimal preparation, everything gets tossed into the pot and dinner is ready in 5 to 10 hours. There are a few things to remember:

• The long time-ranges given in the recipes for cooking (e.g., 8 to 10 hours) take common voltage variations into account. Gear cooking time around your schedule; it is almost impossible to overcook.

• For health safety reasons, chicken should be well chilled before placing it in the pot. Do not begin with a room-temperature or warm chicken. Pots are calibrated to reach a safe temperature based upon beginning with cold food.

• In order to reach the proper temperature, the cooker must be at least half full.

• Don't be tempted to lift the lid before the end of the recommended cooking time. This lowers the internal temperature of the pot, throwing off the timing indicated in the recipe.

• Crockery cooking traps a lot of steam. If excess liquid remains in the pot after cooking, remove the solid ingredients with a slotted spoon and keep warm. Increase the heat setting to high and cook, covered, until the juices have thickened.

• Slow cookers come with detailed instruction booklets. Because pot construction and materials vary, clean your pot only as the manufacturer directs.

• The recipes in this chapter were tested in a 6-quart slow cooker.

Pressure Cookers: Before microwave ovens, pressure cookers were the time-saving secret weapon of many busy home cooks. Unfortunately, "weapon" is not too far from the truth, for those early pots lacked all the safety precautions that now make it virtually impossible to re-create the horror stories we've all heard about food-splattered ceilings—and worse. (This would only happen if the directions were ignored and the lid removed before the pressure was allowed to drop. The design of today's equipment prevents this from ever being able to happen.) Pressure cookers have long been popular in Europe and are now enjoying a well-deserved revival in the United States.

Pressure cookers are available in sizes ranging from 2 to 22 quarts, with 6 quarts being a standard. If desired, some foods can first be browned in the uncovered pot for added flavor. Then add any remaining food to be cooked, cover the pot, and lock the lid in place. Place the covered pot over heat to create steam and thereby build up pressure, then regulate the heat under the pot to maintain the pressure desired. The steam tenderizes the fibers in the food, and the high temperature created within the pot causes the food to cook significantly faster than by other means.

After the dish has cooked for the allotted time, you release the pressure. There are two ways of doing this: With a slow release, you simply turn off the heat and let the pot cool on its own. After anywhere from 5 to 30 minutes, the valve on the lid will indicate when there is no more pressure and it is safe to remove the lid. With a quick release, the hot covered pot is placed under cold running water, which drops the pressure almost instantly. Remember:

• The design of each brand of pressure cooker is unique, so it is imperative to carefully read the manufacturer's instruction booklet concerning operation and maintenance.

• In order to build up sufficient pressure, fill the pot no more than two-thirds full.

- Food inside a pressure cooker is much hotter than food that has been cooked in another manner, so proceed with caution.

- Pressure cookers work magic on dried beans. Just remember that the oil in the bean recipes controls the foam that develops while they cook under pressure. Without oil, the vent in your pressure cooker could clog, causing serious problems. It is very important that the lid and vent always be cleaned carefully after cooking beans.

With these points in mind, you're now ready for the "steamiest" chapter in the book. In fact, since the pressure cooker operates on top of the stove, the clay pot in the oven, and the electric crockery cooker on your countertop, you could make 3 different chicken suppers at the same time! Marvel at the speed with which you can produce Three-Alarm Three-Bean Chicken Chili in the pressure cooker! Savor Slow-Simmered Chicken and White Bean Soup from the slow cooker, and Potted Orange Chicken Orientale from your clay pot. There's only one remaining question: What are you going to do with all your spare time?

Clay Pot Chicken Breasts with Lemon and Olives

Serve this mélange of Moroccan
*flavors on a bed of couscous and garnish with lemon wedges and
fresh oregano sprigs.*   **Makes 4 servings**

4 chicken breast halves on the
   bone (about 2 pounds)
1½ tablespoons lemon juice
1 tablespoon extra-virgin olive oil
1 tablespoon chopped fresh
   oregano or 1 teaspoon dried
3 garlic cloves, minced
½ teaspoon ground cumin
½ teaspoon salt

¼ teaspoon pepper
2 (15-ounce) cans garbanzo
   beans, rinsed and drained
1 (9-ounce) package frozen
   artichoke hearts, thawed
16 medium pimiento-stuffed green
   olives (about ½ cup)
1 small onion, chopped
½ cup chicken broth

1) Trim off any excess fat from the chicken. Rinse the chicken under cold
running water and pat dry. In a bowl or heavy-duty 1-gallon plastic food storage
bag, combine the chicken, lemon juice, olive oil, oregano, garlic, cumin, salt,
and pepper. Marinate at room temperature 30 minutes.

2) Soak the top and bottom of a 3-quart (6-pound capacity) clay pot in cold
water 15 minutes.

3) Combine the garbanzo beans, artichoke hearts, olives, onion, and
chicken broth in the bottom of the clay pot, stirring gently to mix. Arrange the
chicken breasts on top.

4) Cover the pot and place on the middle rack of a cold oven. Turn the
temperature to 450 degrees F and bake 45 minutes. Remove the lid and stir the
vegetables. Bake, uncovered, until the chicken is lightly browned on the outside
and white throughout but still juicy, 5 to 10 minutes. Transfer the chicken and
vegetables to a warm serving platter. If desired, skim the fat from the cooking
juices and pass the juices separately.

Clay Pot Chicken Thighs
with Mushrooms
and Jarlsberg Cheese

A *white-and-wild rice combination makes the perfect base for this sophisticated pairing.*

Makes 4 to 6 servings

10 chicken thighs on the bone
  (about 2½ pounds), skin
  removed
1½ tablespoons extra-virgin olive
  oil
1 tablespoon lemon juice
1 tablespoon chopped fresh
  thyme or 1 teaspoon dried
1 garlic clove, minced

1 teaspoon salt
¼ teaspoon pepper
1 cup shredded Jarlsberg or other
  Swiss cheese (about 4 ounces)
3 cups sliced mushrooms (about
  ½ pound)
3 medium shallots, thinly sliced
½ cup dry white wine
2 tablespoons chopped parsley

1) Trim off any excess fat from the chicken. Rinse the chicken under cold running water and pat dry. In a bowl or heavy-duty 1-gallon plastic food storage bag, combine the chicken, olive oil, lemon juice, thyme, garlic, salt, and pepper. Marinate at room temperature 30 minutes.

2) Soak the top and bottom of a 3-quart (6-pound capacity) clay pot in cold water 15 minutes.

3) Arrange the chicken thighs in a single layer in the bottom of the clay pot. Scatter the cheese over the chicken. Top with the mushrooms and shallots. Drizzle the wine over all. Cover the pot and place on the middle rack of a cold oven. Turn the temperature to 450 degrees F and bake until the mushrooms are tender and the chicken is white throughout but still juicy, 50 to 55 minutes. Using a slotted spoon, remove the chicken and mushrooms to a warm deep serving platter. Skim the fat from the cooking juices and pour the juices over the mushroom mixture. Garnish with the parsley just before serving.

Potted Orange Chicken Orientale

Makes 4 servings

1 whole chicken (about
  3½ pounds)
½ teaspoon salt
¼ teaspoon pepper
1 garlic clove, minced
1 large orange
6 carrots (about 1 pound), peeled
  and cut into 1½-inch lengths

2 medium onions, cut into slices
  ½ inch thick
¼ cup soy sauce
1½ tablespoons brown sugar
2 teaspoons grated fresh ginger

1) Soak the top and bottom of a 3-quart (6-pound capacity) clay pot in cold water 15 minutes. Remove the chicken neck, giblets, and pockets of fat from the chicken cavity and reserve for other uses. Rinse the chicken inside and out under cold running water and pat dry. Rub the cavity with the salt, pepper, and garlic.

2) Grate the zest from the orange. Cut the orange in half and squeeze the juice into a measuring cup (you should have about ½ cup juice). Remove any seeds. Coarsely chop the orange pulp and place in the cavity of the chicken.

3) Place the chicken inside the clay pot and surround with the carrots and onions. In a small bowl, mix the orange juice, soy sauce, brown sugar, and ginger until the sugar dissolves, then drizzle over the chicken and vegetables. Top with the reserved orange zest.

4) Cover the pot and place on the middle rack of a cold oven. Turn the temperature to 450 degrees F and bake 1 hour. Remove the lid and stir the vegetables. Bake, uncovered, until the vegetables are tender and the chicken is lightly browned on the outside and white throughout, about 10 minutes. (The juices should run clear when the thigh is pricked with a fork at the thickest point.)

5) Remove the chicken from the pot, cover loosely with foil, and let stand 15 minutes before carving. Using a slotted spoon, transfer the vegetables to a serving platter and keep warm. If desired, skim the fat from the cooking juices and pass the juices separately.

Garlicky Chicken and Potatoes in a Clay Pot

A *double dose of garlic and the perfume of fresh rosemary makes this aromatic and irresistible.*

Makes 4 servings

1 whole chicken (about
  3½ pounds)
1 teaspoon salt
¼ teaspoon pepper
1 large sprig of fresh rosemary or
  parsley
6 garlic cloves, 2 smashed and
  4 thinly sliced

1 bay leaf
12 small red potatoes (about
  1 pound), cut in half
½ cup chicken broth
2 teaspoons chopped fresh
  rosemary or parsley

1) Soak the top and bottom of a 3-quart (6-pound capacity) clay pot in cold water 15 minutes.

2) Remove the chicken neck, giblets, and pockets of fat from the chicken cavity and reserve for other uses. Rinse the chicken inside and out under cold running water and pat dry. Rub the cavity with the salt and pepper. Place the rosemary sprig, 2 smashed garlic cloves, and bay leaf in the cavity.

3) Place the chicken inside the clay pot and surround with the potatoes. Drizzle with the chicken broth and scatter the sliced garlic over all. Cover the pot and place on the middle rack of a cold oven. Turn the temperature to 450 degrees F and bake 1 hour. Remove the lid and stir the vegetables. Bake, uncovered, until the potatoes are tender and the chicken is lightly browned on the outside and white throughout, about 10 minutes. (The juices should run clear when a thigh is pricked with a fork at the thickest point.)

4) Remove the chicken from the pot, cover loosely with foil, and let rest 15 minutes before carving. Using a slotted spoon, remove the potatoes and sliced garlic to a serving platter and keep warm. If desired, skim the fat from the cooking juices and pass the juices separately. Just before serving, sprinkle the chopped rosemary over the potatoes and garlic.

Clay Pot Chicken with Spicy Potatoes and Tomatoes

A *crisp green salad and a crusty loaf of bread are all that is needed to complete this meal.*

Makes 4 servings

4 chicken breast halves on the bone (about 2 pounds)
¾ teaspoon salt
½ teaspoon paprika
¼ teaspoon pepper
2 (14½-ounce) cans Mexican-style stewed tomatoes, drained and coarsely chopped
1 large onion, cut into ½-inch dice
1 cup corn kernels, fresh or frozen

3 medium red potatoes (about 1 pound), scrubbed and cut into ½-inch dice
½ cup chicken broth
1 (2¼-ounce) can sliced pitted ripe olives, drained
6 tablespoons crumbled feta cheese
2 tablespoons coarsely chopped cilantro

1) Trim off any excess fat from the chicken. Rinse the chicken under cold running water and pat dry. Season with the salt, paprika, and pepper.

2) Soak the top and bottom of a 3-quart (6-pound capacity) clay pot in cold water 15 minutes.

3) Combine half of the tomatoes, the onion, corn, potatoes, chicken broth, and olives in the bottom of a clay pot; stir gently to mix. Arrange the chicken on top. Spoon the remaining tomatoes over the chicken breasts.

4) Cover the pot and place on the middle rack of a cold oven. Turn the temperature to 450 degrees F and bake 45 minutes. Remove the lid and stir the vegetables. Top each chicken breast with 1½ tablespoons cheese. Bake, uncovered, until the cheese has melted, the potatoes are tender, and the chicken is white throughout but still juicy, 5 to 10 minutes.

5) Remove the chicken and vegetables to a warm deep serving platter. Skim the fat from the cooking juices. Pour the juices over the vegetables. Garnish with the cilantro just before serving.

Overnight Chicken Chili

*T*he *last thing at night, stir everything into the slow cooker and you'll be ready to fill those thermoses in the morning.*   ***Makes 6 to 8 servings***

10 skinless, boneless chicken
   thighs (about 1½ pounds)
¾ teaspoon salt
¼ teaspoon pepper
1 (28-ounce) can crushed
   tomatoes with added puree
2 (15-ounce) cans black beans,
   rinsed and drained
2 (15-ounce) cans Great Northern
   (large white) beans, rinsed and
   drained
1 large onion, chopped

1 medium red or green bell
   pepper, cut into ½-inch squares
1 (8-ounce) can tomato sauce
1 (7-ounce) can diced green chiles
1 to 2 tablespoons chili powder,
   to taste
1 jalapeño or serrano pepper,
   seeded and minced
3 garlic cloves, minced
1 teaspoon ground cumin
½ teaspoon dried oregano

1) Rinse the chicken under cold running water and pat dry. Cut into 1-inch pieces and season with the salt and pepper.

2) In a 6-quart electric slow cooker, gently mix together the chicken, tomatoes with their puree, beans, onion, bell pepper, tomato sauce, chiles, chili powder, jalapeño pepper, garlic, cumin, and oregano.

3) Cover and turn the heat setting to low. Cook until the chicken is cooked through and the vegetables are tender, 8 to 10 hours. Season with additional salt and pepper to taste.

Herbed Chicken in a Slow Cooker

*T*his simply delicious supper
deserves a basket of flaky buttermilk biscuits to pass at the table.

Makes 4 servings

1 whole chicken (about
  3½ pounds)
1 teaspoon salt
½ teaspoon pepper
2 tablespoons lemon juice
3 celery ribs, cut into slices
  ½ inch thick
3 carrots, peeled and cut into
  slices ¼ inch thick

2 medium onions, cut into slices
  ½ inch thick
3 garlic cloves, thinly sliced
½ cup chicken broth
1½ tablespoons chopped parsley
¼ teaspoon dried thyme leaves
¼ teaspoon paprika

1) Remove the chicken neck, giblets, and pockets of fat from the chicken cavity and reserve for other uses. Rinse the chicken inside and out under cold running water and pat dry. Rub the cavity with the salt and pepper. Rub the outside of the chicken with the lemon juice.

2) In a 6-quart electric slow cooker, mix together the celery, carrots, onions, and garlic. Place the whole chicken on top of the vegetables and drizzle the chicken broth over all. Sprinkle the parsley, thyme, and paprika over the chicken. Cover and turn the heat setting to low. Cook until the chicken is white throughout but still juicy, 8 to 10 hours. (The juices should run clear when the thigh is pricked with a fork at the thickest point.)

3) Remove the chicken from the pot, cover loosely with foil, and let stand 15 minutes. (Meanwhile, keep the vegetables in the pot until ready to serve.) Carve the chicken and serve with the vegetables.

Crocked Chicken in Creamy Mushroom Sauce

Be sure to offer a loaf of crusty peasant-style bread to soak up this sauce. For a more substantial feast, serve over wide egg noodles. **Makes 4 to 6 servings**

4 skinless, boneless chicken
   breast halves (about
   1½ pounds)
¾ teaspoon salt
¾ teaspoon pepper
¾ cup dry white wine
3 tablespoons tomato paste
½ pound sliced mushrooms
   (about 3 cups)

1 large onion, chopped
2 medium celery ribs, chopped
2 tablespoons brandy
2 garlic cloves, minced
1 teaspoon dried thyme leaves
¼ cup heavy cream
Chopped parsley

1) Turn the heat setting of a 6-quart electric slow cooker to high while you prepare the ingredients. Rinse the chicken under cold running water and pat dry. Cut into 1-inch pieces and season with the salt and pepper.

2) In the crockery pot, whisk together the wine and tomato paste until well blended. Add the chicken, mushrooms, onion, celery, brandy, garlic, and thyme and stir gently to mix. Cover. Reduce the heat setting to low and cook until the chicken is white throughout but still juicy and the mushrooms are tender, 7 to 9 hours. Stir in the cream and increase the heat setting to high. Cook until heated through and the flavors have blended, about 30 minutes. Season with additional salt and pepper to taste. Garnish with the parsley just before serving.

Slow-Fashioned Chicken Noodle Supper

*T**here's something very comforting about a simple dinner like this on a cold wintry night. Serve with a salad of butter lettuce tossed with an herb vinaigrette.*

Makes 4 servings

1 (3½-pound) chicken, cut into
  8 pieces
¾ teaspoon salt
½ teaspoon pepper
1 small onion, chopped
2 cups chicken broth

8 ounces medium egg noodles,
  cooked until barely tender
1 (10-ounce) package frozen peas,
  thawed
2 tablespoons chopped parsley

1) Rinse the chicken under cold running water and pat dry. Season with the salt and pepper. In a 6-quart electric slow cooker, combine the chicken and onion. Pour in the chicken broth. Cover and turn the heat setting to low. Cook until the chicken is white throughout, 8 to 10 hours.

2) Using tongs, transfer the chicken to a clean work surface. Increase the heat setting to high and stir in the noodles.

3) When the chicken is cool enough to handle, pull the meat off the bones and tear into small pieces. Discard the skin and bones. Return the chicken to the pot and add the peas. Cook, covered, stirring occasionally, until the peas and noodles are tender, 30 to 45 minutes. Serve in soup plates garnished with the parsley.

Slow-Simmered Chicken and White Bean Soup

*T*he slow cooker is an effortless way to make full-flavored soups like this. **Makes 6 to 8 servings**

4 chicken breast halves on the bone (about 2 pounds)
1 teaspoon salt
¼ teaspoon pepper
6 cups chicken broth
2 (15-ounce) cans Great Northern (large white) beans, rinsed and drained
2 red potatoes (about ¾ pound), peeled and cut into ½-inch dice

½ pound fresh green beans, cut into 1-inch lengths
1 large onion, chopped
2 medium celery ribs, chopped
2 medium carrots, peeled and chopped
1½ teaspoons dried basil
1 garlic clove, minced
1 (14½-ounce) can stewed tomatoes, coarsely chopped

1) Turn the heat setting of a 6-quart electric slow cooker to high while you prepare the ingredients. Remove the skin and any excess fat from the chicken breasts. Rinse the chicken under cold running water and pat dry. Season with the salt and pepper.

2) In the crockery pot, gently mix together the chicken breasts, chicken broth, canned beans, potatoes, green beans, onion, celery, carrots, basil, and garlic. Cover and cook on high 1 hour. Reduce the heat setting to low and cook until the chicken is white throughout but still juicy, 6 to 8 hours. Using tongs, transfer the chicken breasts to a clean work surface. When cool enough to handle, pull the chicken meat off the bones and tear into small pieces. Discard the bones.

3) Increase the heat setting to high and stir in the stewed tomatoes with their juices. Cook, covered, 10 minutes. Stir in the chicken pieces and cook, covered, until heated through, about 5 minutes. Season with additional salt and pepper to taste.

Chicken with Pressured Black Beans and Rice

This spicy meal is hearty, flavorful, and low in fat. Do not leave out the oil, thinking you'll save on calories; it is needed for successfully cooking the dried beans in the pressure cooker. **Makes 4 to 6 servings**

⅔ cup dried black beans
4 skinless, boneless chicken thighs (about ¾ pound)
2½ cups chicken broth or water
1 medium onion, coarsely chopped
2 medium celery ribs, coarsely chopped
⅔ cup converted long-grain white rice

1 (10-ounce) can diced tomatoes and green chiles, juices reserved
2 tablespoons vegetable oil
4 garlic cloves, minced
1 teaspoon salt
¼ teaspoon pepper
⅛ teaspoon hot pepper sauce
½ cup sour cream
2 tablespoons chopped scallions

1) Rinse the beans in a colander under cold running water. Pick over them and discard any grit. Place the beans in a large bowl or pot and cover with water by at least 2 inches. Soak overnight. Drain and rinse in a colander.

2) Rinse the chicken under cold running water and pat dry. Cut into ¾-inch pieces. In a 6-quart pressure cooker, combine the beans, chicken, chicken broth, onion, celery, rice, tomatoes and chiles with their juices, oil, and garlic until well mixed. Close the lid and lock in place. Place over high heat and bring to high pressure, 10 to 15 minutes. Adjust the heat to maintain high pressure and cook 15 minutes.

3) Reduce the pressure with the quick-release method by placing the cooker in the sink under cold running water to cool the pot. Remove the lid, tilting it away from you to allow the excess steam to escape.

4) Season the chicken mixture with the salt, pepper, and hot pepper sauce. Top each serving with a dollop of sour cream and a sprinkling of chopped scallions.

Three-Alarm Three-Bean
Chicken Chili

Serve this chili with your favorite fixings, such as warm flour tortillas or corn chips, sour cream, shredded Cheddar cheese, and chopped red onion.

Makes 4 to 6 servings

1 cup dried red kidney beans
¾ cup dried pinto beans
¾ cup dried pink beans
1 pound ground chicken
1 large onion, chopped
1 medium red or green bell
   pepper, cut into ½-inch squares
2 tablespoons vegetable oil
1½ tablespoons chili powder

1 or 2 jalapeño or serrano peppers,
   seeded and minced, to taste
6 large garlic cloves, minced
1½ teaspoons ground cumin
1 teaspoon dried oregano
1 teaspoon paprika
¼ teaspoon cayenne
1 (15-ounce) can tomato sauce
2 teaspoons salt

1) Rinse the beans in a colander under cold running water. Pick over them and discard any grit. Place the beans in a large bowl or pot and cover with water by at least 2 inches. Soak overnight. Drain and rinse in a colander.

2) Place the ground chicken in a 6-quart pressure cooker and break into chunks with the back of a spoon. Stir in 7 cups water, the onion, bell pepper, beans, oil, chili powder, jalapeño pepper, garlic, cumin, oregano, paprika, and cayenne until well mixed. Close the lid and lock it in place.

3) Place the pot over high heat and bring to high pressure, about 15 minutes. Adjust the heat to maintain high pressure and cook 15 minutes longer. Reduce the pressure with the quick-release method by placing the cooker in the sink under cold running water to cool the pot. Remove the lid, tilting it away from you to allow excess steam to escape.

4) Stir in the tomato sauce and salt. Return the pot to the stove and cook, uncovered, over medium heat until the flavors have blended and the mixture is heated through, about 10 minutes. Season with additional salt and cayenne to taste.

Quick Chicken Stew with Potatoes and Rosemary

Makes 4 to 6 servings

1 (3½-pound) chicken, cut into
  8 pieces
1 teaspoon salt
¼ teaspoon black pepper
3 tablespoons olive oil
2 medium onions, cut into slices
  ½ inch thick
1 large celery rib, cut into ½-inch
  dice
3 medium red potatoes (about
  1 pound), cut into ¾-inch dice

1 (14½-ounce) can diced
  tomatoes, drained
1 cup chicken broth
1 tablespoon chopped fresh
  rosemary or 1 teaspoon dried
⅛ teaspoon crushed hot red
  pepper
1 (9-ounce) package frozen Italian
  green beans, thawed

1) Rinse the chicken under cold running water and pat dry. Season with the salt and pepper.

2) In a 6-quart pressure cooker, heat the olive oil over medium-high heat. Add the onions and celery and cook, stirring occasionally, until softened but not browned, 3 to 5 minutes. Carefully drain off and discard the excess oil from the pot. Stir in the potatoes, tomatoes, chicken broth, rosemary, and hot pepper. Return the chicken to the pot. Close the lid and lock it in place.

3) Place the pot over medium-high heat and bring to low pressure, 5 to 10 minutes. Adjust the heat to maintain low pressure and cook 16 minutes. Reduce the pressure with the quick-release method by placing the cooker in the sink under cold running water. Remove the lid, tilting it away from you to allow excess steam to escape.

4) Stir in the green beans. Return the pot to the stove and cook, uncovered, over medium heat until the vegetables are tender, 5 to 10 minutes. Season with additional salt and black pepper to taste.

Chicken Gumbo Under Pressure

T*his highly seasoned souplike stew is traditionally served over long-grain white rice.*

Makes 4 to 6 servings

3 skinless, boneless chicken
  breast halves (about 1 pound)
½ teaspoon salt
½ teaspoon pepper
¼ cup vegetable oil
¼ cup flour
1 large green bell pepper, cut into
  ½-inch squares
2 medium celery ribs, cut into
  ½-inch dice
1 medium onion, cut into ½-inch
  dice

3 garlic cloves, minced
4 cups chicken broth
½ teaspoon cayenne
½ teaspoon ground cumin
½ teaspoon dried thyme leaves
¼ teaspoon dried oregano
½ pound okra, cut into slices
  ½ inch thick
½ pound andouille sausage, Cajun
  tasso, or any other spicy fully
  smoked sausage, cut into slices
  ½ inch thick

1) Rinse the chicken under cold running water and pat dry. Cut into ¾-inch pieces and season with the salt and pepper.

2) In a 6-quart pressure cooker, heat 1 tablespoon of the oil over medium-high heat. Add the chicken and cook, stirring, until white throughout but still juicy, 3 to 4 minutes. Remove the chicken from the pressure cooker and set aside.

3) Heat the remaining 3 tablespoons oil in the pot. Gradually whisk in the flour. Cook over medium-high heat, whisking constantly, until the mixture is a rich medium brown, 4 to 5 minutes. (Do not let it burn.) Carefully add the bell pepper, celery, and onion. Reduce the heat to medium. Cook 1 minute, stirring constantly. Stir in the garlic and then the broth, the remaining ¼ teaspoon pepper, the cayenne, cumin, thyme, oregano, and okra. Close the lid and lock it in place.

4) Increase the heat to high. Bring the pot up to high pressure, 10 to 15 minutes. Adjust the heat to maintain high pressure and cook 5 minutes longer.

Reduce the pressure with the quick-release method by placing the cooker in the sink under cold running water to cool the pot. Remove the lid, tilting it away from you to allow the excess steam to escape.

5) Stir in the chicken and the sausage. Return the pot to the stove and cook, uncovered, over medium heat until the flavors have blended and the mixture is heated through, 5 to 10 minutes. Season with additional salt and pepper to taste.

Pressure-Braised Chicken with White Wine and New Potatoes

This simple yet satisfying dinner is always a hit. Serve with fresh warm dinner rolls. **Makes 4 servings**

1 (3½-pound) chicken, cut into
  8 pieces
1 teaspoon salt
¼ teaspoon pepper
2 tablespoons vegetable oil
1 medium onion, chopped
2 garlic cloves, minced
6 small red potatoes (about
  ½ pound), cut in half

½ cup dry white wine
¼ cup chicken broth
1½ teaspoons fresh thyme or
  ½ teaspoon dried
1 (10-ounce) package frozen peas
  and carrots, thawed
Fresh thyme sprigs

1) Rinse the chicken under cold running water and pat dry. Season with the salt and pepper. In a 6-quart pressure cooker, heat the oil over medium-high heat. Add the chicken, in batches without crowding, and cook, turning, until nicely browned on both sides, about 10 minutes per batch. Set the chicken aside as it is browned.

2) Add the onion and garlic to the cooker and cook, stirring occasionally, until softened but not browned, 3 to 5 minutes. Carefully drain off and discard the excess oil from the pot. Stir in the potatoes, wine, chicken broth, and thyme. Return the chicken to the pot. Close the lid and lock it in place.

3) Place the pot over medium-high heat and bring to low pressure, 5 to 10 minutes. Adjust the heat to maintain low pressure and cook 16 minutes. Reduce the pressure with the quick-release method by placing the cooker in the sink under cold running water. Remove the lid, tilting it away from you to allow excess steam to escape.

4) Transfer the chicken to a warm serving platter and cover loosely with foil to keep warm. Leave the potatoes in the cooker but turn them cut side down. Return the pot to the stove and cook, uncovered, over high heat until the juices are reduced by half, about 5 minutes.

5) Reduce the heat to medium and stir in the peas and carrots. Cook, stirring occasionally, until the vegetables are tender and heated through, about 5 minutes. Season with additional salt and pepper to taste. Using a slotted spoon, place the vegetables around the chicken. Pour sauce over all. Garnish with the thyme.

Index

c. and pineapple stir-fry, 56

spicy c. with sweet basil, 43

stir-fried fajitas, 51

stir-fried c. with summer squash, 57

sweet and sour stir-fry, 54

Taipei curry-in-a-hurry, 50

Thai-style c. thighs with peanuts and mint, 58

Yogurt sauce, Indian-spiced c. in, 38

Zucchini

in c. cacciatore, 88

fusilli with c., tomatoes, and, 98

in stir-fried c. with summer squash, 57